DAN BREE

DAN BREEN

AND THE

IRA

JOE AMBROSE

MERCIER PRESS

WHAT YOU NEED TO READ

Mercier Press
Douglas Village, Cork

Trade enquiries to CMD Distribution
55A Spruce Avenue, Stillorgan Industrial Park, Blackrock County
Dublin

© Joe Ambrose, 2006

ISBN: 978 1 85635 5063

10 9 8 7 6 5 4 3 2

A CIP record for this title is available from the British Library

To the Norrises – Michael, Mai, Nora, Josie, Jimmy and Pat.

Mercier Press receives financial assistance from the Arts
Council/An Chomhairle Ealaíon

Printed in and bound by J.H. Haynes & Co. Ltd, Sparkford

CONTENTS

INTRODUCTION

Dan Breen runs like a ragged thread through the history of Ireland in the twentieth century. He helped kick-start the country's War of Independence in 1919; he played a major role in that war and a more uneasy part in the ensuing Civil War. He remains, to this day, one of the most famous and contentious IRA leaders of his generation. He once said, 'The secret of my success is the word republican'.

The Irish may owe him a certain debt of gratitude but the Irish are cranky by nature; they sometimes like to take pot shots at iconic characters like Breen.

The Irish are also a post-colonial people, incessantly told what to do and think by international opinion makers working in publishing, broadcasting and the arts. A colourful and curious array of nay-sayers, soothsayers and academics – not to mention pseudo-scholars fighting their own private Wars on Terror – devote entire Amazon rain forests of paper to debunking some simple facts of narrative history concerning Ireland's War of Independence. They've taken to their task with gusto and occasional aplomb, undermining complex mythologies which have grown up around the likes of Breen, Michael Collins and Tom Barry. Trying to dismantle the reputations of these rural lads of humble origin, they have sought to create post-modern mythologies of their own from which 1916–23 guerrilla leaders emerge as political deviants from some imaginary, civilised, democratic norm, frantically in league with nebulous forces of evil, indifferent to mandate or morality.

The simple storyline and sequence of events to be found in the memoirs, statements, interviews and correspondence of those participating in the 1916–23 IRA campaign, is closer to the truth. Those leaders of what is called the 'Old IRA' emerge from their own testimonies as heroic figures. They undoubtedly saw *themselves* that way. They thought they were 'a grand collection of men'. What did the rest of the people in their country make of them? The answer to that question is as simple as the storyline and does not need the interpolation of researchers or commentators. Those who supported the notion that Ireland would only get independence from England through armed struggle thought them terribly heroic. Those who thought 'freedom' could be achieved by purely democratic means – and those who favoured union with Britain – often thought of them as thugs with blood on their hands. One's assessment of the Tan War leaders has everything to do with one's own political prejudices and nothing to do with the history of that combat.

Dan Breen, more than most others, is regularly filed away under 'Thug with Blood on His Hands'. This is largely because of the ongoing controversy surrounding his first major guerrilla outing as part of the gang behind the Soloheadbeg RIC killings, but it is partially because of the forthright manner in which he defended that gory exploit for the rest of his life. Mary Anne Allis – the aunt of his comrade, Seán Treacy – called him 'Breen the Murderer' until the day she died. Having witnessed Breen's behaviour during the Soloheadbeg clash, Séamus Robinson made a mental note that he was a man who 'should never be put in charge of a fight'. A close relative of my own, who was forever seeing Dan Breen around our family's farmyard when she was growing up, said, 'There was something dirty about that Dan Breen'.

Rumour had it that he was illiterate and couldn't have written his own book. In fact he wrote vigorously and read voraciously. Enemies suggested he was some kind of crypto-fascist, sympathetic to Hitler and opposed to the redistribution of wealth. However, he lent his weight to the left-leaning Republican Congress and, in league with socialist republican Peadar O'Donnell, was active in the anti-Vietnam War movement.

Blame and plaudits were heaped upon Breen all through his life; he accepted the blame and soaked up the plaudits. He said the RIC men he helped kill at Soloheadbeg were, 'a pack of deserters, spies and hirelings' and, 'I would like to make this point clear and state here without any equivocation that we took this action deliberately having thought the matter over and talked it over between us'.

Though he was certainly a radical extremist throughout the War of Independence – and this is his overriding reputation – the Dan Breen who lived on into the era of Kennedy and the Vietnam War was a conciliator and a moderate. Trusted by both sides before and during the Civil War, he did everything in his power to avoid that conflict. One of his initiatives led to a temporary pact between Michael Collins and De Valera which, for a while, looked like it was going to avoid that grim quarrel. He was the first republican politician to take his seat (and the oath of allegiance) in the Free State parliament.

Soloheadbeg remains a political and historical hot potato. It also remains a substantial turning point in the history of modern Ireland. It forced the hand of nascent Dublin-centred urban power elites within Sinn Féin, the IRB and the IRA. Breen's other colourful involvements – like the fights at Knocklong and Ashtown Road – are less controversial manifestations of an unquenchable generational spirit.

My paternal grandfather – who was also in the IRA but who took the opposing side in the Civil War – used to say that Breen's memoir, *My Fight For Irish Freedom*, was the book in which the word 'I' was used the most often in the English language. That the book is full of self-aggrandisement, bombast and bias is beyond question. That it sometimes plays hard and fast with the facts is likely. Séamus Robinson – who was unduly prejudiced against Breen – called it 'The Great Tipperary Hoax'.

My Fight for Irish Freedom made Dan Breen one of the permanent heroes of the revolution. Well paced, unremitting, a *Boy's Own* story, it stands alongside *Speeches from the Dock* and *Jail Journal* as a bible of Irish nationalism. Compared with the literary – but bookish – guerrilla writings of Che Guevara or Ernie O'Malley it might seem thin gruel but it was written as propaganda. It is hugely successful, Homeric, propaganda.

Dan Breen certainly didn't win his war single-handed and the ego-driven style of his ghost-written book is not replicated in his 'Statement to the Bureau of Military History' in Dublin. The Breen who emerges from that recollection was very political, very realistic and impressively harsh. That Dan Breen painted a picture of a collective Tipperary leadership which was determined, all on their own if needs be, to remove Ireland from the British empire.

In February 1919, the Third Tipperary Brigade of the IRA – the sons of small farmers and labourers – issued a proclamation instructing the British to quit south Tipperary under pain of death. The decree was greeted with derision by the British and with disapproval by the Dublin republican establishment. Exactly three years later, the last British soldiers left south Tipperary. What happened in between is a significant story – at that moment in time Britain seemed as invincible as the United States seems today. The efforts of disenfranchised people wielding a hodgepodge of muskets, mud bombs and captured weapons seemed as hopeless in 1919 as similar efforts by Vietnamese peasants seemed in the 1960s or as the Palestinian resistance seems now.

A number of punctilious historians have chronicled the untamed activities of the Third Tipperary Brigade. Desmond Ryan wrote a hagiographical study of Seán Treacy and the Third Brigade which had the merits and demerits of being both written and published while the majority of the participants were still alive. An tAithair Colmcille Conway wrote a typically forthright and partisan history of the brigade from 1916 right through to the end of the Civil War which had enthusiasm and unique access to brigade members about it. In more recent years Joost Augusteijn has deconstructed the story of south Tipperary IRA Volunteers with efficiency and academic rigour. Augusteijn sups from the same revisionist trough which feeds an undeniable intellectual blackguardism but he does know what he is talking about.

The real story of Dan Breen and the IRA – told here for the first time in the words of those who participated in it – is considerably more moving and more interesting than the myth. This book seeks to recalibrate the story of Dan Breen, the Big Four (Breen, Treacy, Robinson and Seán Hogan) and the Third Tipperary Brigade so that the other players come into the spotlight. Breen operated in the middle of a group of noteworthy individuals who felt it was 'the decree of history' that they would stand or fall together. This is their story too.

The myth of the Big Four doesn't bear close examination. Séamus Robinson – whose many polemics, rants and recollections have been seized upon by sloppy revisionists anxious to prove what a bad lot the Tipperary IRA were – was a decidedly hesitant combatant, disliked by Michael Collins and distrusted by many members of the Third Tipperary Brigade. His 1950s written attacks on Breen, informed by retrospective bitterness and jealousy which bordered on the irrational, are worth noting but are unreliable. Seán Hogan, younger than the others, led the Second South Tipperary Flying Column but was regarded by his comrades as being unfit for leadership. His capture by the RIC – which led to the Knocklong rescue – was just one of many incidents wherein his careless, brainless or irresponsible behaviour put himself and his companions in danger. Breen and Treacy were what they seemed to be – gutsy, spirited militants willing to risk everything for what they saw as a high ideal. Other Tipperary activists – such as Eamon O'Duibhir, Maurice Crowe or Dinny Lacey – were probably more deserving of the fame which was heaped upon Robinson and Hogan. Nevertheless, the legend of the Big Four acted as a stirring call to arms during 1919 when the outcome of the War of Independence was far from clear.

When I was tramping with my mother through the roads and boreens of Tipperary in 1981, speaking to Dan Breen's contemporaries and working on a small book about him, Ireland was in many ways identical to the country he fought in and for. That has all changed now. The events of ninety years ago seem terribly remote. Few Irish people now know what a haggard* is or what real hunger feels like. 'Oró 'Sé do Bheatha 'Bhaile', the song which the Third Tipperary Brigade sang as they marched through the Galtee Mountains, is today best known as a track on a Sinead O'Connor album. Many of the principles and aspirations which those people fought for seem neither here nor there. This makes the job of explaining what happened, whom it happened to and why it happened at all, crucial.

JOE AMBROSE

www.joeambrose.net

1

SEÁN TREACY AND DAN BREEN

In Tipp, landlords' estates had been broken up and there were many
small holdings. The men were more independent; the houses neater and
better built than in other counties I had visited. The men were tall and
quiet; they had a great deal of purpose and were dependable.

Ernie O'Malley, *The Singing Flame*

Dan Breen was born in the village of Donohill, Tipperary, probably on 11 August 1894, to Daniel Breen, a labourer, and Honora Breen, née Moore, a midwife from a district close to Doon in Co. Limerick. Daniel Breen died of blood poisoning at the age of sixty, when Dan was a small child.

Breen had a clear memory of his father's coffin being brought into the room in which he was waked. The women keened so much that they were sent down to the kitchen. In *My Fight for Irish Freedom*, Breen spoke warmly of a father he scarcely knew: 'I remember one sunny day when he took me up by the hand and led me through the fields. When I got tired he lifted me on to his shoulders and brought me home pick-a-back.'

In his subsequent statement to the Bureau of Military History he was more dismissive. He said his father's people had been fenians but the impression gained was, 'that he belonged to a type of fenian who's more talk than anything else … I had heard it said of the people that he resembled that they were great fellows for talking and drinking and doing very little else after that but, on the other hand, I suppose there was little they could do in their day.'

Breen's family was a large one; his siblings were Laurence, Mary, John, Winifred, Catherine, Patrick and Laurence Junior, who was known as Lar. The older Laurence died when Dan was four years old.

'We were not blessed with a lot or worldly goods,' remembered Breen. 'My mother was a midwife and so when my father died she had to work very hard to support us. The family was generally a young family [at the time of Daniel's death], I being about six and there was another brother after me who was only in his cradle but, nevertheless, we lived happily there. My mother was a hard worker and thrifty and contrived to make ends meet.'

Honora Breen spent some of her widow's pittance purchasing popular paperback books containing the rebel writings of Wolfe Tone, Robert Emmet and the other icons of Irish nationalism. Breen reckoned that the women were the most impressive people in the south-west Tipperary society from which he came. He said it was the women who promoted fenian ideals: 'The men of my father's generation had apparently drifted into a system of what we would call public house debate as their only contribution to the national movement of the time, but it is the women who kept alive the traditions of the past and handed those things on to my generation.'

'Dan regularly spoke about his mother,' said Clonmel Fianna Fáil activist Ernie Hogan. 'The other men and women who were active at that time talked about her too, saying that she was formidable. She entirely egged Dan on in his political activities. By general agreement, she was more "extreme" than Dan – she was one of those great old fenian ladies. Little learning perhaps but a great spirit. The Tan War cost her dearly and she ended up nearly destitute.'

Life in Tipperary towards the end of the nineteenth century was tough. Brutalising rural poverty was never far away, in the midst of the ascendancy architecture of the big towns and big houses. Between 1891 and 1911 Tipperary lost fourteen per cent of its population. The towns didn't decline as dramatically as the countryside – and some even prospered. Tipperary town, the nearest sizeable settlement to Donohill, had three creameries. One of these, owned by Cleeve's Condensed Milk Company, employed 300 people, including a large percentage of women.

'We were not too well off in those days,' Breen told Jim Maher in 1967, 'and our neighbours were only barely above the poverty line too. We mostly ate potatoes and milk. Sometimes we had salted pork for our dinner, but we hardly ever ate fresh meat. We also ate much cabbage and turnips.'

Tom Garvin in *Nationalist Revolutionaries in Ireland*, points out that society had just recently emerged from agrarian feudalism and was 'only partly affected by urban culture, denied political power by the colonial establishment, without any self-assured intelligentsia other than the priests and the young men whom the priests had educated.'

Watching what was happening to neighbouring small farmers and noting the poor prices they got for their produce, Breen developed a lifelong interest in the politics of land and property. Childhood political memories included the brutal eviction of a nearby cousin who died homeless on the side of the road.

'I was a socialist in outlook,' he told Jim Maher, 'I was never a communist; I never believed in communism but I was a strong socialist. I did not see any possibility of a socialist state, because I knew that the establishment would step in and crush it. I never understood why any man with a family, denied work, should let himself and his family go hungry. I always felt that it was the duty of a man to provide for his family and if he couldn't get enough food by honest means, he should take it.'

The great political debate of his childhood concerned the Boer War (1899–1902), a key conflict which saw the emergence of jingoism, Winston Churchill and concentration camps. People around Donohill were pro-Boer and Breen overheard their daily discussions concerning the war's progress.

Like most boys of his social class, Breen enjoyed a good primary education at the hands of teachers who, in addition to the British curriculum, taught the Irish language and the story of Ireland seen through the prisms of ancient mythology or more recent history. Fenians and other separatists took their place in a colourful pantheon alongside Cúchullain,* Oisín* and the Fianna.* The children heard a great deal about the Famine (1845), with England's assumed role in it brought up at every opportunity.

The schoolboy Breen could never understand 'why a million people were allowed to starve to death in Ireland in the Great Famine in an agricultural country, when Irish wheat and other foodstuffs were allowed out of the country. I wanted to take the people of Ireland out of serfdom. I did not want to enrich them but I wanted them to have a better way of life. I wanted to take the people out of the slums and bad living conditions and give them decent lives – lives as good as they would get anywhere else in the world.'

Most of the nationalist-minded primary teachers – later to

play an important role in the emergence of the IRA – were members of the Tipperary-founded Gaelic Athletic Association (GAA) and of its companion organisation, the Gaelic League – a reasonably altruistic organisation dedicated to the revival of the Irish language.

The school in Donohill was an architecturally unimpressive affair, recalled by Breen as a, 'drab two-storey building with no playground for the pupils.' Girls were educated upstairs, boys on the ground floor. One teacher in particular had a significant impact on Breen: a Kerryman called Charlie Walshe. Walshe, who was subsequently a Fianna Fáil TD and mayor of Dublin (as Cormac Breathnach), was employed by the Gaelic League to teach Irish in the rural districts. 'He did relief work in several of the schools in our district,' Breen said. The stimulating and confrontational Charlie Walshe also taught Seán Treacy (vice-commandant, Third Tipperary Brigade IRA), Dinny Lacey (commandant, Third Tipperary Brigade, IRA Flying Column) and Seán Hogan (Third Tipperary Brigade, IRA Flying Column).

'We learned about the Penal Laws, the systematic ruining of Irish trade, the elimination of our native language,' said Breen. 'He told us about the ruthless manner in which Irish rebellion had been crushed. By the time we had passed from his class, we were no longer content to grow up "happy English children" as envisaged by the Board of Education.'

Another seditious travelling teacher who passed through the neighbourhood was Thomas Malone (aka Seán Forde) who would eventually return to that part of the world as an organiser from Volunteer GHQ and who would lead former pupils like Breen and Treacy into fierce battle.

Breen left school at the age of fourteen and did a number

of farm labouring jobs before going to work as a linesman for the Great Southern Railway in 1911 when he was seventeen. This work brought him around the country and meant that he was out of Donohill at a time when his pal and neighbour, Seán Treacy, began organising the Irish Volunteers.*

Treacy's father, like Breen's, died young. This led to Treacy's family moving in with their maternal aunt, Mary Anne Allis. Allis was a hard-nosed small farmer who wanted Seán to concentrate on farming, which he was good at, and to avoid the covert militant circles towards which he was drawn. She regarded Breen as a bad influence on her nephew and, in later years, would refer to him as 'Breen the Murderer'. She, understandably, hoped that Treacy would 'make his way in the world'. Breen – who disliked her intensely – said she wanted Treacy 'to work like a nigger on the small farm that they had and which could scarcely make a living for them.'

In 1911, Treacy, aged sixteen, joined the IRB and began attending Irish language classes at Eamon O'Duibhir's home in Ballagh; the two usually spoke to each other in Irish after that. Between 1914 and 1917, he continued to attend Irish classes at the Tipperary Technical School.

'Seán was taller,' wrote Ernie O'Malley. 'An easy smile or a long grin showed his teeth. Glasses gave him a quiet appearance; he had a good strong-thrusting chin. His humour was dry enough. He dealt with men quietly. I envied him his ease; yet he never allowed slackness to pass by.' Breen said that Treacy was, 'away ahead of anything one might expect to meet in a country district. He had vision and to him nothing was impossible.' Another contemporary, Seán Horan, described Treacy as 'a silent and also a sincere worker.'

20

Treacy was also a keen, if tone deaf, singer. One of his favourite songs, 'Oró 'Sé do Bheatha 'Bhaile', concerned Grace O'Malley, the west of Ireland pirate queen, and it celebrated armed youth who would root the foreigner out of Ireland:

> *Tá Gráinne Mhaol ag teacht thar sáile,*
> *Óglaigh armtha léi mar gharda;*
> *Gaeil iad féin 's ní Gaill ná Spáinnigh,*
> *'S cuirfid siad ruaig ar Ghallaibh.*

Dan Breen once said that 'Seán Treacy tried to form himself on the image of Michael O'Dwyer of Wicklow; the rebel who held out in the Wicklow hills after 1798. Treacy loved everything that was Gaelic. He spent much time studying the Irish language when he was young. And he fancied himself as a singer, although he had a voice like a crow. Often he nearly drove me insane listening to him trying to sing "Oró 'Sé do Bheatha 'Bhaile" but it sounded to me like "A Nation Once Again"!'

Breen's job as a linesman paid reasonably well, allowed him to see the country, familiarised him with the workings of the railway system, and meant he was stationed at Inchicore in Dublin for quite long periods of time. He witnessed at close quarters the 1914 Lock Out and the baton-wielding repression meted out to the striking workers. No matter where he was stationed, he kept an eye on developments back home.

'Dan took a shine to Dublin, to city living, like many a country man before him,' said IRA man Seán Dowling. 'When I got to know him it was apparent that he knew the place well, had clearly cycled and walked all over the city back when he was working at Inchicore. He set great store by the Dublin working-classes, regarded them as natural supporters of our cause. Treacy liked Dublin too, liked the trams and the cinemas, but Treacy always wanted to get home to Tipperary. Dan wanted to linger and, as it turned out, he ended up lingering in Dublin for good.'

'The IRB circle to which we belonged was centred at Doon,' noted Breen. 'There were very few people around our part of the country that could be relied upon and so we had to cycle eight or nine miles to attend those circle meetings. Packy Ryan of Doon was the centre of the circle and it was at Ryan's that I first met Seán Mac Dermott who, I believe, was on some kind of an organising mission around Munster. It may have been at Kilmallock because Packy Ryan also had a place there ... We were only ordinary members and, being little more than boys, we were just looked upon as handy messengers and suchlike, so that we did not know about what was going on except what we could see for ourselves.'

At the time of the 1916 Rising, Breen was working on a line near Kilmallock, Co. Limerick, as part of a gang of 150 men. Out of that number, only he and one other man were militant separatists. 'When I came home for Easter,' he said, 'Treacy told me he expected a rising to take place on Easter Sunday but when the cancellation messages were received he told me about them and I went back to my work beyond Kilmallock ... Having heard further messages of the Rising in Dublin I returned home again on Tuesday until the Friday of that week ... he [Treacy] was away from home and, so we learned since, was cycling around from one centre to another trying to urge the Tipperary Volunteers to take action to support the fighting in Dublin.'

The collapse of the Rising, particularly Tipperary's insignificant role in it, confused and angered Treacy and Breen but strengthened their youthful resolve. When they'd studied the history of 1798, they'd wondered why the entire country had not risen up. They were sure that when *their* turn came, they'd strike out in a meaningful manner but, Breen said, 'wrong orders and not knowing what to do kept us from taking part … We made up our minds then that when anything like that would happen again we would be part of it no matter what.'

In the aftermath of the Rising debacle, the Donohill revolutionaries whipped themselves up into a frenzied campaign of recruitment and organisation. A headquarters/meeting place was eventually established at Lisheen Grove, not far from Tipperary town.

'Hitherto we had looked to the townspeople as being more in touch with things and perhaps as countrymen we suffered some sense of inferiority,' said Breen. 'Now however, for some reason, after the Rising the townspeople were more inclined to look to us and so conditions were reversed. Treacy and I went about to all the towns like Tipperary, Cahir and other places about there and urged the reorganisation of the Volunteers.'

Seán Horan, terribly demoralised by the failure of the Rising, ran into Treacy in Tipperary town. He'd left work with the intention of travelling to Dublin to fight but, on Easter Monday night, in Tipperary, he'd found out that there wasn't a hope of getting into the city.

'Seán [Treacy] got to know my mind,' said Horan. 'It was through Dan Breen that I met him. Before Seán and I parted that evening he invited me to Lisheen Grove, two and a half miles from Tipperary town … The Lisheen Grove officers decided to go to the outside parishes and get companies working. So Seán Treacy went to Mount Bruis. Dan Breen and I went to Solohead and Cappawhite. We paraded each company and when we had finished we went to Mount Bruis. When we met with Seán he was drilling about twenty ladies. I remarked to Seán, "What will you put the ladies to doing, Seán?" "Well," said he, "they'll be put to something. They can carry dispatches".'

2

EAMON O'DUIBHIR AND PIERCE MCCAN

The main Volunteer organisers in south Tipperary were Eamon O'Duibhir, Seán Treacy and Pierce McCan. Joost Augusteijn, in *From Public Defiance to Guerrilla Warfare*, claims the RIC didn't detect evidence of the existence of Irish Volunteers in south Tipperary until the end of 1915: 'By January 1916 the RIC … had become aware of 380 Irish Volunteers in five units … one in Ballagh under Eamon O'Dwyer, one under Pierce McCan around Cashel, one in Fethard, one in Clonmel under Frank Drohan and one near Tipperary town under Seán Treacy.' None of these men saw the coming revolution through to its conclusion. Treacy and McCan died, and Drohan and O'Duibhir eventually withdrew from the fray, dismayed by the realities of guerrilla warfare.

The RIC talked in their reports of a local farmer – O'Duibhir – who had contacts with Dublin and who was busy organising malcontents into some sort of separatist movement. O'Duibhir (1883–1963) was a burly, complex, good-humoured man valued throughout his area, busy putting the Sinn Féin policy of economic autonomy into practice. He sold insurance on behalf of Irish insurance companies, encouraging people who sought cover to withdraw their business from the then-dominant English firms. By 1916, O'Duibhir, a farmer/entrepreneur, more prosperous than most other leaders of the nascent south Tipperary IRA, was county centre for the Irish Republican Brotherhood (IRB).

There were thirty-two such individuals in the country, one for each county. The county centre's job was to recruit suitable new members, to organise the spread of IRB branches throughout the county, and to encourage the infiltration of other "Irish Ireland" organisations by IRB members.

The IRB – a secret society disapproved of by the catholic church and by many republicans – was the lineal successor to the clandestine fenians. The fenians' 1867 rebellion had been a dismal failure, but surviving old fenians – like Roscarbery's O'Donovan Rossa and Tipperary's John O'Leary – had a profound influence on the 1916 leaders and on young IRA organisers like Breen and Treacy. Between 1908 and 1914, the IRB revived itself and was the chief organising force behind the 1916 Rising. It subsequently infiltrated the Irish Volunteers. Michael Collins became its leader in 1919. Their oath asserted:

'In the presence of God, I, … , do solemnly swear that I will do my utmost to establish the independence of Ireland and that I will bear true allegiance to the Supreme Council of the Irish Republican Brotherhood and the government of the Irish Republic and implicitly obey the constitution of the Irish Republican Brotherhood and all my superior officers and that I will preserve inviolable the secrets of the organisation.'

It was Seán Treacy who administered this oath to Dan Breen. Breen later quit the IRB when they attempted to rein in his activities. Ernie O'Malley – never a member – afterwards accused the IRB of undermining the ideal of the republic.

O'Duibhir said that his interest in separatist thinking had been awakened early in the century by Irish language lessons in the *Weekly Freeman's Journal*. The learning of Irish, in chronic decline all over rural Ireland, suggested to thoughtful men like

O'Duibhir that they belonged to a place which was culturally unlike England.

Through a locally organised Irish class he came to know a lot of like-minded individuals. In 1908, they started a Sinn Féin club in the parish. Politically and openly, these people eventually involved themselves in the anti-ranch campaign, the anti-conscription movement and in the broad range of farmers' concerns.

The November 1913 trip to Munster by IRB man Seán Mac Dermott – which had such a profound effect on Breen – is often mentioned as the event which triggered the start of covert paramilitary action in south Tipperary. He spoke at the Tivoli Hall in Tipperary town. Seán Fitzpatrick – later in the flying columns with Dinny Lacey and Dan Breen – talked of a speech which 'aroused the dormant, but by no means dead, national spirit of the townspeople ... a shot in the arm for Irish Irelanders amongst his audience.'

Through Gaelic League connections Eamon O'Duibhir had already met the passionate, intense, young Seán Treacy, busy organising Volunteers in Tipperary town – ten miles away from O'Duibhir's base at Ballagh. It fell to O'Duibhir – a natural leader, educator and organiser – to call a meeting in Ballagh, at the time of the MacDermott visit, at which an Irish National Volunteer company was formed. This company then assisted others in getting units going. Irish language classes arranged by O'Duibhir played a key part in recruiting men and women to parallel organisations like the Irish National Volunteers, the IRB and Sinn Féin. Thomas Ryan – eventually a member of the Second South Tipperary Flying Column under Seán Hogan – said that it was these classes which awakened his interest in

Irish history and, by implication, since the two things are rarely separated, in Irish politics.

Joost Augusteijn says that by 1914 there were 2,000 Volunteers in south Tipperary.

In those early days Pierce McCan (1882–1919) was as important as Eamon O'Duibhir. McCan was rich, the son of wealthy catholics whose fortune had been made in Australia. The McCan family owned several homes and Pierce grew up on a 1,000 acre estate, complete with a mansion house residence, at Ballyowen, near Cashel. He became a progressive farmer whose methods were admired by his less prosperous neighbours. He formed a Volunteer company from the men working on his land and was able to train and drill them there clandestinely.

McCan, who was to be involved in nearly every nationalist organisation, was educated like an English gentleman. As a child he had a private tutor, Southendy, who was brought over from England. After that he was sent to Rockwell College and then Clongowes, as if his family was determined to send him on a grand tour of the best catholic boarding schools Ireland had to offer. In 1900, he visited France, before going to Denmark to look into Danish farming methods. By 1909 he was, like the entire revolutionary generation, caught up in Irish language classes. Love of the language caused him to holiday in the west of Ireland where he developed an affinity for the wild windy vistas of the Aran Islands and the highlands of Donegal.

Through the ubiquitous Gaelic League (by 1908, there were eighteen Gaelic League branches in Tipperary) McCan knew many IRB and revolutionary people in Dublin. In 1914, together with Frank Drohan and Rockwell College Irish teacher, Séamus O'Neill, McCan organised a Volunteer group in Clonmel. Perhaps because of his class background and because he had once shared a platform with Parliamentary Party leader John Redmond, many thought that McCan was more of a Home Ruler than a Sinn Féiner but he was especially close to Arthur Griffith, the founder of Sinn Féin.

When Redmond urged the Volunteers to join the British army and participate in the Great War – effectively signing the death warrant of the once-illustrious Parliamentary Party – the Volunteer movement split in September 1914. The vast majority supported Redmond and became the National Volunteer organisation. McCan refused to back Redmond and the Doon Volunteers were the only corps in Tipperary whose members refused to join the British army. 'This was probably because Seán Treacy and Dan Breen were members of it,' suggests Tipperary historian, John Shelley.

When the greatly depleted Volunteers regrouped at Dublin's Abbey Theatre in October 1914 – with wary conspiratorial IRB figures like Bulmer Hobson, Tom Clarke and Seán Mac-Dermott playing prominent roles – Pierce McCan and Eamon O'Duibhir led the small Tipperary delegation.

Two years later, during the 1916 Rising, McCan made every effort to bring the Tipperary Volunteers into the rebellion. He was arrested and sent from his patrician mansion to the gloomy Arbour Hill prison where he witnessed the execution and burial of men who were his friends and comrades.

In a memoir of his incarceration he described what he saw in the prison yard: 'At one end a huge trench was dug … the full length of the end of the yard. A very small portion of the upper end of this grave, for grave it was, had been filled in. Under this filling lay the corpses of Pearse, MacDermott and the rest …

who had been shot. Full boxes of quicklime were thrown on the ground nearby. There were a few empty ones there also, the contents of which had been doubtlessly thrown upon the dead bodies of my friends and fellow Volunteers of a few days ago.'

McCan was subsequently sent to Frongoch interment camp, a university for the revolution about to happen. When he got back to Tipperary the first thing he did was re-start Irish language classes. He played an active role in setting up branches of Sinn Féin in Clonmel, Rosegreen, Killenaule, Tipperary and Carrick-on-Suir.

By December 1917, he was encouraging boycotts against state institutions like crown courts and the RIC. He called on people to turn to republican alternatives and emphasised the ultimate necessity of violence.

On 19 May 1918, McCan was arrested for his part in the fabricated German Plot and jailed in England. He was one of the large number of Sinn Féin MPs elected in 1918 – his constituency was east Tipperary – who were unable to attend the meeting of the first dáil because they were incarcerated. In prison he contracted the flu bug then sweeping through Europe and died in March 1919. His funeral, a choreographed political affair, was one of the events which restored the fortunes of the embryonic IRA after Soloheadbeg. Michael Collins and Harry Boland* were just two of the republican luminaries who participated in the Dublin end of the funeral at the pro-cathedral – an occasion said to have been attended by 10,000 mourners.

SÉAMUS ROBINSON ARRIVES IN TIPPERARY, 1917–19

In the years immediately before the War of Independence, young people in Ireland enjoyed new freedoms, both socially and politically. New ways of life were emerging all over Europe. The old order was collapsing, undermined by the traumas of the Great War. The men and women who fought the War of Independence enjoyed music, dancing, movies, late night shindigs and situations in which three was a crowd. Many narratives of the Third Tipperary Brigade find them departing from dances at 4 a.m., having discussions in bars, leaving cinemas, or eagerly roaming the countryside – day and night.

James Malone, theoretically an Irish teacher in Tipperary in 1917, nurtured the cultural and social changes which went hand in hand with an emergent militancy. 'I spent one night per week in each place,' he told Uinseann MacEoin. 'There was an Irish class from eight to nine-thirty, a céilí from nine-thirty to eleven-thirty and I drilled the Volunteers for an hour after that. There were classes for the schoolchildren in the evenings. I spent the day travelling the countryside, trying to set up new branches or representing the Volunteers or the Brotherhood. Some branch held a big céilí every Sunday night, as a rule and in the fine weather there was a feis somewhere on a Sunday. Well known speakers from Dublin and from other places attended the feises for the purpose of exhorting the people.'

Patrick 'Lacken' Ryan, a man subsequently remembered in memoirs by Ernie O'Malley and Dan Breen, described the early days of Volunteer organising: 'On a night in the early summer of 1917 I attended a meeting which was held in a place called Downey's Barn at Cramps Castle, Fethard. This meeting was called for the purpose of organising an Irish Volunteer company in Fethard and district … The meeting itself was a small one, as for obvious reasons only a selected number of men were invited to attend. I should say, however, that there were about twenty men present, all of whom agreed to become members of the Volunteer organisation.'

Trustworthy men in inactive areas who were thought to be willing and able to start a company were approached. Joost Augusteijn discovered that the obvious starting point – when initiating a company or setting up a battalion – was often a relative.

The enrolment of Thomas Ryan from Ballylooby was a prime example of relatives recruiting one another. Ryan was related to Seán Treacy by marriage and was an obvious choice when Treacy was looking for a local contact to set up the Volunteers in his district. Ryan had always been involved with what might be regarded as 'improving' activities. An accomplished athlete with the GAA, he played football for Tipperary at county level and was subsequently a member of the Tipperary team playing at Croke Park on Bloody Sunday. At one stage, legend has it, he was offered £8 a week to play soccer for Glasgow Celtic. In 1914, he was captain of the local Irish National Volunteer company but, as a result of the split in the National Volunteers, was not involved in 1916.

'Some time about April 1917 Seán Treacy made a few trips to the locality and suggested the organising of a Volunteer unit there,' said Ryan. 'On his second visit to us, he gave us an outline of the organisation and generally encouraged us, pointing out what should be done and how to do it. As a result of Treacy's visit, the battalion was formed with Ned McGrath as the battalion commandant. I was vice-commandant. This was really the beginning of my career in the Volunteer movement. Following Treacy's instructions, we set to work from then on to organise companies in the surrounding parishes, to appoint officers for these and to direct their training.'

At the start of 1917 Eamon O'Duibhir had obtained a loan and bought Kilshenane House and farm, with a view to using it as a base for Gaelic League, Sinn Féin and Volunteer activities. During his Easter Week-induced internment in England he had met a Belfast man called Séamus Robinson who had trouble finding work after his release from prison. Robinson had played a considerable part in the Rising, having been in charge of the farthest outpost from the GPO on Sackville Street, holding the Hopkins and Hopkins shop which looked out over O'Connell Bridge. From that vantage, he was face to face with the full might of the British response to the GPO insurgency. His building was one of the last to be evacuated despite heavy British gunfire. O'Duibhir, in prison, noted Robinson's obvious sincerity and capability. After their release he invited the firm catholic to come and live at Kilshenane as an alleged farm labourer. In fact, Robinson's job was to help manage the Volunteers.

'Robinson arrived some day in January 1917, in the midst of a snow storm,' said O'Duibhir. 'He had with him a small black travelling bag that we got to know very well and to associate with him. As a farm worker he made up for his lack of knowledge by his honesty, hustle and zeal. He certainly worked as hard as he could and left nothing undone that he could do and in addition to all that he was a very gentlemanly man.'

In August 1917, O'Duibhir was arrested for the second time, sent to Cork jail, court-martialled and sentenced to two years. He was transferred to Mountjoy where he went on the first of many hunger strikes, protests which did permanent damage to his health: 'Some of the principal men of the movement in Co. Tipperary were in prison with me, Seán Treacy and Séamus O'Neill in particular. As far as the organisation was concerned, I need not have worried, for Robinson, although new to the place and unknown, had stepped into the gap … we had a housekeeper at Kilshenane and now, when I was taken away and Robinson was left in charge, the P.P. of Knockavilla was not at all satisfied that it was proper to have this young lady in charge of the house with a crowd of young men, some of whom he did not know, in particular Robinson. I am sure Robinson must have been amused at the time over this, because certainly no more proper man could be found than the same Robinson.'

Conditionally released in November 1917, O'Duibhir made a moderate but threatening speech in front of a crowd of 200 people who met him at the railway station when he got home to Tipperary. He said that their collective idea was to make British rule in Ireland impossible and that he believed they would achieve this without firing a shot. If necessary, he went on, they would adopt active resistance.

This notion that the Volunteers could put 'impossible pressure' on the British without resorting to *actual* violence was shared by other Volunteer leaders such as Cathal Brugha.

A few weeks later, the RIC recorded a more bellicose O'Duibhir in front of ninety people: 'That the Volunteers policy today was the same as that for which the Manchester Martyrs died – complete separation from England – that the young men should train and make themselves efficient and ready to act their part when the time came. As surely it would come, as the men of Easter Week did. That no one should be afraid to die as there was nothing about it to be afraid of. That it was far easier to die on the battlefield than on the scaffold or in prison. That at the present time there was a great movement afoot to secure the independence of Ireland by "passive resistance" which was all very well in its way. But it was necessary that this movement should have the support of rifles and machine guns. That they had them already and were still getting them. That at the present time the only enemy they had was England ... that they should take no notice of the laws i.e. the laws of a political character dealing with drilling and such like. They should not mind the police as no one was afraid of the police now ... that they should ignore the law courts and set up their own arbitration tribunals ... that the police if they were sensible men should now throw in their lot with their fellow countrymen in their struggle for freedom and not be on the side of the enemies of their country as heretofore.'

Patrick Ryan provided an account of O'Duibhir and Robinson's rifle-gathering techniques: 'This soldier got off the train at Goold's Cross on furlough ... We got in touch with Séamus Robinson who was in Kilshenane with Eamon O'Duibhir and I located this soldier. Eamon O'Duibhir was at home from gaol, so the two O'Keefes and I went with three lads from Knockaville to Kilshenane and they wanted to put disguises on their faces ... Eamon O'Duibhir was inclined to tell them that it was too dangerous. Séamus Robinson went with us. We had a sort of an old .32 and one round of ammunition. Con Keefe had another gun and he had a strange round of ammunition. Séamus Robinson had a .22 Smith and Wesson automatic. This soldier home on furlough got married and he was more or less on his honeymoon in a house. They were all gone to bed. I went to one room. There were four huge bloody men in two beds. I took a squint but I couldn't see any sign of a rifle but I heard Con's voice ... Con had it. I handled the rifle and the fellows in the room were made very aggressive by this. I told these fellows that I'd have to blow out their brains. I said we were soldiers of the Irish Republic doing our duty ... Séamus was delighted with the gun and we came out onto the road. Séamus Robinson fired the rifle and when he had the gun in his hand I thought it would make an awful report to frighten them, but all it did was to make a ping.'

Another of the 1916 survivors, who'd once been a Donohill Gaelic League teacher, now re-established contact with Treacy and Breen and got to know Robinson. Thomas Malone (whose brother, James, was busy cycling all over the county attending dances, teaching Irish and training Volunteers) had just been elected to the army council with IRB support. He had been sent, early in 1917, to west Limerick – a GHQ man – to knock the local Volunteers into shape. Padraic O'Farrell describes Malone as being 'an astoundingly successful leader'. Aware that the south Tipperary men were better organised and motivated than most other units, he took an interest in what they were up to.

Malone said: 'They were a grand collection of men. Eamon O'Duibhir of Ballagh, Dan Breen, Ned Reilly, Séamus Robinson, Paddy Kinnane, Jimmy Leahy, Joe McLoughlin and Micksey Connell of Thurles, most of them to become well known in the fight afterwards … We planned to ambush and disarm four RIC guarding a boycotted farm. That was two years before Soloheadbeg. We lay in wait, Paddy Kinnane, Breen, Treacy and myself, but they did not come at the right time. We raided Molly's of Thurles and carried away eight boxes of gelignite.'

Early in 1918, O'Duibhir got the job of organiser of the Irish National Assurance Society, for which he recruited hundreds of agents and got a good business going. Kilshenane operated as a live-in semi-collective with Volunteers being given both employment and cover as farm workers or insurance salesmen.

O'Duibhir and his circle set about collecting arms throughout Munster, buying them in Dublin or grabbing them off the RIC whatever chance they got. Thomas Ryan held up a British officer using a carved wooden fake gun and got a Webley .45. Another time he stole a revolver from an RIC man who was courting in a park. Big houses were methodically raided, their hunting rifles seized in the name of the Irish Republic. This resulted in a motley – sometimes useless – arsenal, said by Ernie O'Malley to include British long and short Lee-Enfields, police carbines, Lee-Metfords, single shot Martini-Henris, Sniders, Remingtons, Winchesters, German, Turkish or Spanish Mausers, French Lebels, American Springfields, old flint muskets and muzzle-loading Queen Annes. There were also Webley, Colt, and Smith and Wesson revolvers. There were not too many machine guns but they had gunpowder, gelignite and dynamite.

In March 1918, a confrontation arose between the RIC

and the Volunteers on the streets of Tipperary town. The cause of the confrontation was the trial, at Tipperary courthouse, of Seán Duffy and Tom Rodgers on charges of drilling a few days previously. Duffy, in particular, was a well-known local Volunteer.

Breen was in charge because Treacy was locked up in jail. A few days before the trial Breen sent out orders that as many men as possible from the battalion area were to mobilise at 11 a.m. in the market yard, Tipperary, on the day of the trial, carrying hurleys or stout sticks. About 200 men turned up.

'The men were divided into two companies, Dan taking charge of one and I of the other,' said Maurice Crowe. 'We marched to the courthouse, Dan's party leading and, on our approach, the RIC, under District Inspector Brownrigg, drew a cordon across the road between St Michael's church and the courthouse gate. Dan halted his company near the cordon and my party halted at St Michael's Road, opposite the church.'

The two men began to drill their Volunteers. Since Rodgers and Duffy were being tried on drilling offences, this was an overtly political action.

'The district inspector asked us to stop drilling,' continued Crowe. 'We refused, so the RIC got an order to draw sticks and at this time it looked as if there would be a clash. But the District Inspector saw that the Volunteers were determined and under perfect discipline. The police put back their batons and sent for the military.

'Our scouts gave warning of the approach of the military. Dan immediately gave the order to march and we proceeded down St Michael's Road for some distance and halted. The RIC laughed as they thought we had taken to flight, but they were soon to find out otherwise; instead we held a council of war.

'The military, armed with rifles, had by now arrived and took up positions in Maguire's (stonecutters) Yard opposite the courthouse, some in the courthouse yard, others above and below the courthouse in St Michael's Street. We had by this time divided our whole party into four sections and, at a blast of the whistle from Dan Breen, we came back on the double.

'Dinny Lacey took charge of one of the new sections. Lacey got round to the back of the courthouse. Paddy Deere, who took charge of the other, took up a position above the courthouse, near the Convent Cross. My party went to the back of Maguire's Yard and Dan Breen took up his old position, thereby surrounding the RIC and the military.'

Crowe recalled that the officer in charge had a sense of humour and laughed at being cornered. The Volunteers went into the courthouse and made 'a laughing stock' of proceedings. When the case was over they marched away from the courthouse to the local market yard where they were dismissed by Breen.

The British army and the RIC may have been mildly amused by this exercise in toy soldiers but the more sober amongst them would have noted the fact that what confronted them that day was, assuredly, some kind of organised opposition which was being carried out along military lines.

A few local people were forced to support the rebels whether they wanted to or not. One volunteer claimed, 'It was decided by the battalion or by the brigade headquarters to place a levy on each farmer of five shillings per cow for every cow he owned. The farmers were notified beforehand of the amount of their levy. When we called to collect some paid up at once, saying we were great boys and deserving of support. With others it was not quite so easy and in some cases it was necessary to seize and sell cattle for the amount due. In the latter cases only the amount of the levy was retained and the balance of the money was returned to the former owners of the cattle … A portion of it was handed over to the local branch of the White Cross organisation and the balance of it was forwarded to brigade headquarters.'

Around October 1918, people began to call the Volunteers 'the IRA'. At a meeting overseen by Richard Mulcahy from GHQ, the Third Tipperary Brigade of the IRA took shape. Eamon O'Duibhir became assistant quartermaster under Dan Breen. 'There was some opposition to Dan Breen as quarter-master,' O'Duibhir said. 'It came from the southern end of the county and those delegates said that I was doing the work and why not I be appointed quartermaster. I thanked them for their attitude but said that Dan Breen was the man and I agreed to be assistant brigade quartermaster.'

Séamus Robinson was appointed commandant in a manoeuvre masterminded by Séan Treacy in cahoots with Breen. Treacy was appointed vice-commandant.

'Treacy had arranged that Robinson should be appointed brigade commander to suit his own purpose,' Breen later claimed. 'He wanted a sort of yes-man or a stooge as we would call it now, in the position and we thought that Robinson would serve this purpose.'

Breen said that Treacy reckoned the two of them were 'too unknown and unproved to carry any weight in Tipperary and it must be remembered that a man who had the label of being one of the Volunteers who fought in 1916 was still a hero to us all in 1918.'

Breen and Treacy – having discussed things between themselves – had, prior to the meeting, travelled to Kilshenane to check Robinson out. They liked what they saw and on a subsequent visit offered him the position. In *My Fight for Irish Freedom*, Breen wrote that they: 'asked Séamus if he would agree to become commandant of our brigade. I well remember the night on which we called. We found him milking a cow and our acquaintance with him was so slight that we addressed him as Mr Robinson. Treacy kept on talking to him while he continued with his milking. When he had finished milking the cow, we expected that he might stand up and talk to us, but he took his bucket of milk and walked away, saying over his shoulder as we followed him that he would do whatever we wanted him to do, but that he could not afford to idle as he might lose his job.'

Breen's contention that Robinson was not really in charge is borne out by events and by the opinion of Thomas Ryan: 'I have no direct personal knowledge of the circumstances of the appointment of Robinson … but from what I knew of Treacy, I imagine that it was he who supported if he did not propose Robinson for the appointment. When Treacy lived he was looked upon by all the officers and men of the brigade as the actual power, even though he did not choose to hold the appointment of brigade commander. At brigade council meetings which I attended, though Robinson might preside, it was Treacy who dominated and directed matters and it was therefore to Treacy that we looked for leadership in action.'

'Whenever Treacy was present, he was in charge,' said Breen.

Ernie O'Malley, in *On Another Man's Wound*, said, 'Robinson was pudgy and took short steps, which were hard on my long stride. Brown eyes helped a grin when he played on words; he liked to pun even to the limit of our groans. He had a slight, clipping, speech which came from Belfast, a stout stubborn underlip, sparse hair on a high round forehead.'

Robinson, a serious-minded methodical man, a fretter and a worrier, was an obvious outsider in south Tipperary. His Belfast family had been active in fenianisn and, as a result of enforced political exile, many members (including his father) were born in France. They were people who worried a great deal about being excommunicated because of their fenian activities.

Robinson felt that there was a 'zeal of the convert' aspect to the deeply religious catholic ethos in which he grew up. His great-grandfather – though a nationalist – had been a protestant, indeed a grand master of the Orange Order. Robinson's grandfather, when he left the fenians because he dreaded excommunication, swore that he would never shave again until Ireland got its freedom. Portraits showed him with a long, exuberant beard. Robinson's parents were Parnellites, convinced that the British empire was invincible. When he showed an enthusiasm for 1798 centennial commemorations happening in Belfast he was told: 'It would be lovely if it could be done but your grandfather failed and your great grandfathers failed, all better men than you ever can hope to be and besides England has become much stronger and is just as ruthless.'

Breen and Treacy were hard-nosed wild spirits and may, in Robinson's eyes, have seemed somewhat uncouth fellows. An ardent catholic, Robinson's views were neither inclusive nor egalitarian. He later wrote to Frank Gallagher that the IRA members of his generation were, 'the normal, natural (common) sensible people in Ireland. All others must be objected to as in some degree abnormal, unnatural: that, because we youngsters were normal, that is without a taint of heresy or near heresy, natural or theological, we were Irish separatists.'

The somewhat less exotic citizenry of south Tipperary – many of whom would never have travelled far from home other than on a day trip to local cities like Limerick, Waterford or Cork – eventually found Robinson hard to take. He regularly prefaced his many expressions of opinion with phrases like 'as they say in France'.

Even the cosmopolitan and sophisticated Ernie O'Malley – Munster's sons of the soil had serious misgivings about *his* obvious erudition and intelligence too – sometimes found Robinson difficult to take. 'Séamus had little sense of direction even in day time and in country he had travelled through many times,' he wrote in *On Another Man's Wound*. 'He believed that he had a good memory for country. At crossroads there would be a discussion varying in degree of banter, helplessness or annoyance. Séamus would assert that this particular road was the way or short cut. He was always ready to debate the rightness of his way. The result was always the same. Seán [Treacy] and I sat on a bank or lay hidden to watch his short form walk out of sight. We knew he would return when he discovered his mistake to advance extenuating circumstances, or we might not meet him till night time.'

During October 1918 Treacy and Breen established them-selves in the Tin Hut, the house from which they would soon launch the Soloheadbeg attack. Tadgh Crowe, due to be involved in Soloheadbeg, passed much of that year on the run: 'I spent most of my time away from home, especially at night time. Dan Breen and Seán Treacy were then also on the run and Breen and I spent some weeks together on organising work … Later that year Treacy and Breen set up what I might call their headquarters in an unoccupied house commonly known as the Tin Hut … It was roughly about four miles from my home in Solohead and about half a mile from Treacy's farm at Soloheadbeg.'

In the same month, Eamon O'Duibhir was charged in connection with the German Plot and imprisoned again in England: 'The news came to me of the Soloheadbeg fight and opinion was very much divided amongst the prisoners as to whether the thing was right or wrong. Séamus O'Neill and myself, having a very good idea of the parties that were involved in it, took the side of the Volunteers but the majority of the prisoners did not seem to think that it was a very good thing to happen.'

IRELAND UNDER A MICROSCOPE – MILITANT ATTITUDES TOWARDS THE RIC

If the people became armed and drilled, effective police control would vanish. Events are moving. Each county will soon have a trained army far outnumbering the police and those who control the volunteers will be in a position to dictate to what extent the law of the land may be carried into effect.

Inspector General, RIC, 1914

Between 1919 and 1922, 490 RIC men were killed by the IRA. The RIC were predominantly catholic, though there tended to be fewer catholics in the higher ranks; some were native Irish speakers. Many survivors stayed on in Ireland, usually adopting diplomatically low profiles in a society which saw them as remnants of a failed regime. Some of their fellow countrymen, like Dan Breen, saw them as, 'a pack of deserters, spies and hirelings'.

Ernie Hogan remembered: 'I had this pal when I was young in the 1950s – he was in Fianna Fáil with me – and his father had been RIC. I knew the dad well – he was a decent enough old character. He'd clearly done very well for himself and farmed a large holding in the Cahir area. I remember when he died in the mid 1960s that his death notice in the *Irish Independent* mentioned the fact that he was "ex-RIC". Some people were amazed at his family's effrontery, their lack of embarrassment about his previous existence. RIC men were supposed to be "invisible". I have no doubt that there was a stigma attached to being ex-RIC in Tipperary.'

The armed RIC was always perceived as being the physical manifestation of British rule in Ireland. The British army came out of their barracks when serious suppression was demanded but it was the RIC who did the day-to-day political policing which got up the noses of both moderate and extreme separatists.

'The Peeler and the Goat', a song written in Bansha, a village on the road between Tipperary town and Cahir, was hugely popular in south-west Tipperary when Breen and Treacy were growing up. In the pre-radio era of sing-songs and crossroad entertainments, it was a favourite with the youths of the IRA. The ballad lampooned the RIC by celebrating the attempted arrest of a goat in Bansha; it was apparently based on a real incident, during which the RIC took some troublesome goats into custody:

As Bansha peelers were, one night,
On duty a-patrolling, O,
They met a goat upon the road
Who seemed to be a-strolling, O,
With bayonets fixed they sallied forth,
And caught her by the wizen, O,
And then swore out a mighty oath
They'd send her off to prison, O,
'O, mercy, sirs,' the goat replied,
'Pray, let me tell my story, O,
I am no Rogue or Ribbonman,

No Croppy, Whig or Tory, O,
I'm guilty not of any crime
Of petty or high treason, O,
And I'm sadly wanted at this time,
For 'tis the milking season.'

The Irish Constabulary Act of 1822 had established the Irish Constabulary. Amongst its first duties – during the Tithe War – was the forcible seizure of tithes (payments made by the community for the support of the anglican clergy) from the catholic majority and the presbyterian minority populations.

In 1848, they demonstrated their adroit taste for suppression by putting down the Young Irelanders' rebellion. The fenian rising of 1867, marked by attacks on isolated police stations, was suppressed with ease because the police had infiltrated the fenians with spies and informers.

'The constabulary started off as the Irish Constabulary,' said IRA member Martin Walton, 'but, for their zeal during the fenian rising, Victoria graciously gave them the term "Royal". And they were the eyes and ears.'

By 1901, Ireland contained approximately 1,600 barracks and some 11,000 constables. The majority of the lower ranks in rural areas were of the same social class, religion and general background as their neighbours. For this very reason they were usually transferred far away from their home areas so that social and familial connections with the local community were broken. Through their enforcement of tens of thousands of evictions in rural Ireland and their harassment of land league leaders, the RIC became deeply unpopular with the majority catholic and nationalist population during the nineteenth century. By 1916, they'd gained some general level of begrudged acceptance.

It was this very normalisation of relations which goaded the republicans who saw them as enforcers of an unwanted union with Britain.

With the establishment of the Free State, many RIC men went north to join the RUC. As a result, the original RUC was forty per cent catholic. This fell to eight per cent, as those men reached retirement. Some RIC members joined the gardaí – such men had assisted the IRA in different ways. Many retired, the Free State having agreed to pay their pensions. Others, faced with threatened or actual violent reprisals, fled to Britain.

Seán Kavanagh, who gathered intelligence from RIC informers for Michael Collins, said that, outside of Dublin, the real army of occupation in the years leading up to Soloheadbeg was the RIC, which was armed and semi-military in structure: 'The RIC provided accurate information on every Volunteer company in the country outside of Dublin, while the members of the political wing of the "C" division of the DMP [Dublin Metropolitan Police] reported in detail on every prominent Volunteer in Dublin. After the Rising it was those "political" detectives who identified and selected the leaders for court-martial and summary execution or long sentences of penal servitude.'

Martin Walton said that: 'The country was studded at the time with small police barracks every few miles … You couldn't travel from Dublin to Swords – that's about a distance of seven miles – without going into three RIC outposts and everybody passing up and down the road was noted carefully. In fact when Augustine Birrell, who had been the chief secretary here during the Rising, when he was questioned about the activities of the revolutionaries, he said that the Royal Irish Constabulary had

Ireland under a microscope.'

Michael J. Costello (Fianna Éireann) said: 'When I was a little scut growing up in Cloughjordan I was never frightened by the RIC. They seemed to a young child to be a civilised enough body of men but we knew too that it was the RIC who'd played a major role in suppressing the fenians. It was the RIC who'd supervised evictions in the bad old days. When I was a child it was commonplace for our parents' generation to chat with RIC men in the public house or to pass the time of day with them on the street. 1916 changed all that. On the one hand, a lot of the people grew swiftly alienated from all manifestations of British rule. On the other hand, the RIC themselves became more shifty or suspicious. After Soloheadbeg the more superior men amongst them knew that the game was up and either got out or like Jerry Maher or David Neligan – two fine brave men – made themselves known to, and put themselves at the disposal of, the IRA. Eventually – by the time of the Truce – the RIC had just filled up with bowsies and blackguards. Soloheadbeg was tough. The two RIC killed that day may have been the embodiment of the British empire with two feet on the ground in Tipperary but, as I understand it, they were two harmless enough fellows – armed harmless enough fellows of course. It was a tough call and I'm glad I had no part in it. Dan Breen and Seán Treacy had their own attitude to things, their own solutions. They were their own men and, therefore, they got the whole thing going.'

James Malone, a member of the east Limerick Flying Column (the first of the flying columns) said the RIC, 'were the eyes and ears of Dublin Castle. As long as they remained, British power remained. East Limerick and Tipperary Three

were the brigades that commenced the policy of winnowing
them out.'

SOLOHEADBEG

*If Dan Breen and Seán Treacy had waited for a course in Sandhurst
in 1919, there would have been no revolution in Ireland.*
Peadar O'Donnell

God help poor Ireland if she follows this deed of blood!
Monsignor Ryan, St Michael's church, Tipperary

It was a very small affair compared to later developments.
Séamus Robinson

On Tuesday, 21 January 1919, between 12.30 p.m. and 1 p.m.,
two RIC constables were ambushed by eight Volunteers under
the command of Seán Treacy, near Soloheadbeg Quarry, close
to the homes of Treacy and Dan Breen.

On the same day the Sinn Féin MPs elected in the 1918
British general election – which saw Sinn Féin eclipse the Parliamentary Party amongst Irish nationalists – met in Dublin's
Mansion House. They styled themselves Dáil Éireann, issued a
Declaration of Independence, adopted a provisional constitution
and issued a rather progressive Democratic Programme. Professor Michael Hayes subsequently pointed out that this much-
celebrated first dáil took place, 'within the jurisdiction of an
empire that then had millions of men under arms and had

firmly entrenched and long established organs of government in Ireland'. But, as Charles Townsend says in *The British Campaign in Ireland*, in 1919 the Republic served by the Volunteers was, 'still a different thing from that represented by Dáil Éireann'.

Constables James McDonnell and Patrick O'Connell – the victims at Soloheadbeg – were, with loaded rifles, escorting a horse drawn cart containing a consignment of gelignite from Tipperary military barracks to Soloheadbeg Quarry, where gelignite was needed for blasting purposes. Constable McDonnell, aged fifty-six, came from Belmullet, Co. Mayo. He was a widower with seven children. Constable O'Connell, from Coachford, Co. Cork, aged about thirty, was single. They were accompanied by two civilians, south Tipperary county council employees Patrick Quinn and Edward Godfrey.

The Volunteers who ensnared the small convoy were: Paddy O'Dwyer, Seán Treacy, Séamus Robinson, Dan Breen, Seán Hogan, Michael Ryan, Paddy McCormack and Tadgh Crowe. According to Paddy O'Dwyer, seven of the eight men were armed with revolvers while Treacy carried a small automatic rifle.

Séamus Robinson later claimed that Treacy and his girl-friend, Mai Quigley, had visited him at Kilshenane shortly after Christmas 1918. The purpose of their visit – he said – was to tell him about the imminent delivery of gelignite and to get his permission for the attack. According to Breen, Robinson was not in Co. Tipperary at this time, having been released from Belfast Jail roughly around the end of the year. 'It was the middle of January before we saw him in Tipperary,' said Breen.

Robinson maintained that, 'After tea the two of us [Treacy

and Robinson] went out to the haggard where he told me of the gelignite that was due to arrive at Soloheadbeg Quarry in three weeks time ... he added that there would be from two to six guarding the cart, that they would be armed and that there was the possibility of shooting. "Good," said I, "go ahead but under the condition that you let me know in time to be there myself with a couple of men from the local battalion ... men with whom I would go tiger hunting".'

Robinson claimed that Treacy asked him if they should get permission for the action from Volunteer GHQ in Dublin and that he (Robinson) replied, somewhat jesuitically, 'It will be unnecessary so long as we do not ask for their permission. If we ask we must await their reply.'

Breen saw things differently, showing a degree of contempt for Robinson in his recollection: 'Robinson was not consulted about this ambush or about the plan for it, or about a number of other things like that which were arranged. He was never told about it as something that was being done. Treacy and I had decided that we were going to shoot whatever number of police came along as an escort with this gelignite, but we did not tell Robinson anything about this. It was not a matter of distrusting him or anything like that, but we felt that it did not concern him and that he did not have to know about what our intentions were ... We had the full intention of not alone taking the gelignite they were escorting, but also of shooting down the escort, as an assertion of the national right to deny the passage of any armed enemy.'

Tadgh Crowe took up the story: 'On Tuesday, 14 January 1919, I attended the fair in Tipperary town and called on Maurice Crowe ... and collected from him some ammunition for a revolver which I had at the time. In accordance with instructions, I reported that night to Mrs Breen's (Dan's mother) cottage at Donohill. I met Breen and Treacy there and the three of us went to the Tin Hut at Greenane … We were joined at the hut during the night by Séamus Robinson and Seán Hogan.

'Maurice Crowe, Paddy McCormack (then an Irish teacher in Dundrum), Paddy O'Dwyer from Hollyford, Michael Ryan, Arthur Barlow and Con Power reported next day. During the days that followed there were changes in personnel. On account of their business in life, some were unable to remain for more than a day or two and there were days when Brian Shanahan, Ned O'Reilly, Dinny Lacey and Seán O'Meara were with us.'

Maurice Crowe told Desmond Ryan that on 15 January the conspirators risked bad luck when they interfered with a nearby moat (a large mound of earth) which, according to legend, was home to malevolent fairies: 'Seán Treacy and Arty Barlow went out to cut some bushes to make a fire from a moat near at hand. Someone remarked that it was not right to cut any wood off a moat, to which Seán replied, "Ah, sure the fairies won't say anything to us for trying to keep ourselves warm." The following morning Seán got a breakfast ready at seven o'clock. Some of us were dozing around the fire while others slept on the remains of two beds in the room – this was a disused house. He called several times that the breakfast was ready but the lads were slow in coming. When they did come they had no milk as Seán had consumed the tin of condensed milk. Of course there was general disapproval to which Seán replied, "This will show you that Volunteers must be punctual, even at breakfast!"'

'During our conversations around the fire there were divergent views as to what the strength of the escort would be and various suggestions were made about the best method of holding them prisoner after they were disarmed and until the gelignite was got safely away,' said Tadgh Crowe. 'We assumed all along that the police would surrender and put up their hands and I am certain that none of us contemplated that the venture would end in bloodshed and loss of life.'

'It was laid down as an order,' said Robinson, 'That if only two RIC should accompany the cart they were to be challenged but if there were six of them they were to be met with a volley as the cart reached the gate.'

Paddy O'Dwyer was the lookout whose job it was to warn the group when the gelignite and its guardians were leaving Tipperary: 'For five or six days I cycled to Tipperary each morning and returned each evening with nothing to report. At night-time we went to the vacant house on Hogan's farm to sleep ... A week-end intervened and on the Saturday morning I cycled home to Hollyford for a change of clothing and cycled back to Solohead on the Sunday night.'

'After a week's wait the whole affair ended suddenly and in a tense atmosphere,' said Tadgh Crowe. 'My recollection is that the two RIC men armed with carbines were walking behind the horse and cart when it came into the ambush position. There were several shouts of "Hands up!" I myself shouted that command at least two or three times. I saw one of the policemen move up to the cart and crouch down beside it. From the position he took up and the manner in which he was handling his carbine, I was satisfied that he was going to offer resistance.'

'The hot-headed tension of Breen made it even more vitally important that Treacy should be collected and cool in order to be able to deal with any emergency,' said Robinson. 'One could depend on cool riflemen. Small arms in the hands of men in their first fight, no matter how cool these men may be, are almost useless at a range of more than two yards.'

Paddy O'Dwyer said he was with Robinson 'on the extreme left-hand side of the position, about twenty-three or thirty yards away from what I will call the main party of six and the arrangements were that Robinson and I were to get out on to the road when we heard the others call on the men with the cart and the escort to stop and put up their hands, the idea being that if they did not halt, Robinson and I would be in a position to stop the horse and cart.'

'Seán Treacy and Dan Breen at the last exciting moment started to insist that they should be allowed to rush out,' said Robinson. 'Breen seemed to have lost control of himself, declaring with grinding teeth and a very high-pitched excited voice that he'd go out and face them.' Robinson later claimed that, right there and then, he made a mental note that Breen 'should never be put in charge of a fight'.

Séamus Robinson felt that, 'The RIC seemed to be at first amused at the sight of Dan Breen's burly figure with nose and mouth covered with a handkerchief; but with a sweeping glance they saw his revolver and O'Dwyer and me … they could see only three of us.'

'Hearing Dan Breen and Seán Treacy shouting, "Halt, put up your hands!" Robinson and I immediately started to get out on to the road,' said O'Dwyer, 'and almost simultaneously either one or two shots rang out. I distinctly remember seeing one of the RIC men bringing his carbine to the aiming position and working the bolt and the impression I got was that he was aiming at either Robinson or myself. Then a volley rang out and that constable fell dead on the roadside. I am not certain whether it was that volley or the previous shot, or shots, which killed his companion.'

'I fired three shots at him,' admitted Tadgh Crowe. 'One was ineffective and the other two got him in the arm and back. About the same time, either one or two shots were fired from the gate where Seán Treacy was positioned and the other constable fell, shot through the temple.'

'The driver of the cart and the county council ganger were, naturally, very frightened,' said Paddy O'Dwyer. 'Dan Breen spoke to them and told them that nothing was going to happen to them. One of these men, Godfrey, knew both Breen and Treacy well and I imagine that Flynn must have known them too. On Breen's instructions, Tadgh Crowe and I collected the two carbines belonging to the dead constables. Breen, Treacy and Hogan then drove away the horse and cart with the gelignite.'

'I took the belts with the pouches of ammunition and hand-cuffs off the dead policemen,' said Tadgh Crowe. 'Treacy, Breen and Hogan drove away on the horse and cart with the gelignite and Paddy O'Dwyer and I took the RIC men's carbines and hid them together with the belts, pouches of ammunition and handcuffs in a ditch about half a mile from the scene of the ambush. O'Dwyer and I then parted, he to go back home to Hollyford and I went to Doherty's of Seskin.'

'Seán Treacy had made all the arrangements for disposing of the gelignite,' remembered Robinson. 'Dan Breen and Seán Hogan mounted the cart, Breen, standing up with the reins, whipped the horse and away they went clattering on the rough road. I had thought that Dan Breen, who had worked on the railway, would have known the danger of jolting gelignite that was frozen … the weather was very cold. Hogan told me afterwards that he tried to caution Dan but either he couldn't hear him or he put no "seem" to it.'

According to Breen: 'Séamus Robinson did not know of the police being shot that day until he was nearly at home in Ballagh. He was at a point about 300 yards from where the shooting took place and, though he heard the shots I suppose, he did not see the effect of them. It was Robinson himself who told me afterwards that himself and McCormack, one of the other men who were engaged with us, had nearly arrived at Ballagh on their way home when McCormack told him that the two police were dead and that this was the first he heard of anyone being killed.'

In his 'Statement to the Bureau of Military History', a sealed account of events left behind for future generations, Breen went out of his way to repeatedly claim that he and Treacy set out to kill RIC men at Soloheadbeg: 'I would like to make this point clear and state here without any equivocation that we took this action deliberately having thought the matter over and talked it over between us. Treacy had stated to me that the only way of starting a war was to kill someone and we wanted to start a war, so we intended to kill some of the police whom we looked upon as the foremost and most important branch of the enemy forces which were holding our country in subjection. The moral aspect of such a decision has been talked about since and we have been branded as murderers, both by the enemy and even by some of our own people, but I want it to be understood that the pros and cons were thoroughly weighed up in discussions between Treacy and myself and, to put it in a nutshell, we felt that we were merely continuing the active war for the establishment of the Irish Republic that had begun on Easter Monday, 1916. We felt there was grave danger that the Volunteer organisation would disintegrate and was disintegrating into a purely political body ... and we wished to get it back to its original purpose ... We also decided that we would not leave the country as had been the usual practice, but that, having carried out this act of war, we would continue to live in the country in defiance of the British authorities ... The only regret we had, following the ambush, was that there were only two policemen in it instead of the six we expected, because we felt that six dead policemen would have impressed the country more than a mere two.'

In *My Fight for Irish Freedom*, which appeared while many of those involved in the ambush were still alive and while Breen was an active politician, he chose his words more prudently: 'We would have preferred to avoid bloodshed but they were inflexible.'

Witnesses later claimed to have seen a cart being driven furiously by two masked men with a third in the back. As Breen put it in *My Fight for Irish Freedom*, their 'career of real excitement' had just begun.

SOLOHEADBEG: REACTIONS AND
CONSEQUENCES

Rewards of £1,000 for the capture of Breen and the others were quickly offered. Wanted posters featuring photographs of Breen were displayed outside RIC barracks all over the country and descriptions of Breen, Hogan, Robinson and Treacy were printed in the RIC's *Hue and Cry*.

Joost Augusteijn says that the RIC were so spooked by the killings that they suddenly perceived threats and enemies all over the place. 'Everywhere it is pervaded with young men who show hostility to any form of control,' the south Tipperary RIC county inspector reported in January. 'Imbued with Sinn Féin propaganda and possessed of arms and ammunition, they are a danger to the community.' In April 1919, the RIC reported that seventy per cent of the people were 'in sympathy with the attackers'.

Paddy O'Dwyer boasted: 'Whilst I was purchasing a newspaper in a shop in Hollyford the following day [22 January], two RIC men came to the door and stood there. One of them appeared to be taking a keen interest in me and was looking me up and down. Opening the newspaper, I read aloud, with assumed amusement, the story which it carried of the shooting of the constables at Soloheadbeg on the previous day. The policemen remained at the door listening and as I wanted to give them the impression that I was in no way perturbed by their presence, I then read out the leading article, which, in no uncertain terms, condemned the shooting. Any suspicions which the RIC men may have entertained of my connection with the affair were apparently allayed, for when a friend called me I left the shop without being in any way molested by them.'

Lord French, the lord lieutenant who enjoyed almost dictatorial powers at the height of the Tan War, famously said that the mere commission of the Soloheadbeg crime had dealt a severe blow to the Sinn Féin organisation.

An tÓglach, the organ of the Volunteers, edited by Piaras Béaslaí – a close confidante of Michael Collins who'd been intimately involved in drafting the constitution of the first dáil – weighed in behind the attackers. On 31 January, the paper stated that Volunteers were justified in 'treating the armed forces of the enemy – whether soldiers or policemen – exactly as a national army would treat the members of an invading army.'

Richard Mulcahy, chief-of-staff at GHQ when the attack took place, later confided to his son that, 'bloodshed should have been unnecessary in the light of the type of episode it was.' Mulcahy, a stickler for detail, order, and discipline, conceivably saw the unauthorised fight as a direct challenge to – or sign of contempt for – his personal military authority. He reckoned that Dr Kinnane, the archbishop of Cashel, who 'many years after told me that he had regarded Soloheadbeg as part of official policy ... withdrew his mind from such things and concentrated entirely on the religious and the moral aspect of his responsibilities and work. When, later, a monument was being erected at Soloheadbeg to mark the episode, he intimated to those concerned that he did not wish any priest in his diocese to be associated with it and that as far as the parish priest was concerned, into whose parish the president, Seán T. O'Kelly, was going for the occasion of the unveiling, he was to receive the president with all due courtesy, but not to be associated with the official proceeding.'

Mulcahy's tart disapproval was voiced privately to his son in the early 1970s, towards the end of his life. When writing 'Chief of Staff – 1919' shortly beforehand for the 1969 *Capuchin Annual*, he was rather more circumspect, saying that Soloheadbeg fell, 'naturally into the general position of local initiative in reaction against aggression.' In the same essay he, more acrimoniously, claimed that, 'no cure for the malaise in the army command in south Tipperary could be found in military manuals or in any order that could be issued from the general headquarters staff.'

Mulcahy wasn't always so cautious. Three years before Solo-headbeg, while incarcerated in Frongoch Camp after the 1916 Rising, he made a speech to his fellow internees: 'To bring a revolution to a satisfactory conclusion we need bloodthirsty men, ferocious men who care nothing for death or slaughter or blood-letting. Revolution is not child's work. Nor is it the business of saint or scholar. In matters of revolution, any man, woman, or child who is not for you is against you. Shoot them and be damned to them!'

Mulcahy ended his political days as a Fine Gael opponent of Dan Breen in the Tipperary South constituency and some rancour concerning that situation – Mulcahy never once got more votes than Breen – may have coloured his attitude retro-spectively.

Tom Garvin, in *Nationalist Revolutionaries in Ireland*, cites a Tipperary IRA leader who said that the real effect of the war sparked off by the Soloheadbeg ambush had been the intimidation of informers and of civilians generally, rather than the breaking of British power: 'The RIC were at sea when they pimped   and pried yet could not gather scraps of news through their ordinary sources in pubs and fairs, or by talking to men who had met men who came in from the country; or by talking to pub owners. The once prolific sources of talk-supply were drying up. In Tipperary due to Solohead the people were warned – afraid of talking – and so they kept their minds to themselves and their neighbours. As a result the south Tipperary people did not talk much.'

Jerome Davin, a stalwart of the Third Tipperary Brigade recalled: 'One morning a party of military visited Rosegreen. This was unusual at the time [early 1919], so with a Volunteer I went to the village to see what they had been doing. I found that they had put up a large notice in the village offering a reward for information which would lead to the arrest and conviction of the persons concerned in the shooting of the two RIC men at Soloheadbeg. From a good friend and solid Irishman, the late Ned O'Neill, I got a sheet of notepaper, on which I wrote in block letters the following words: "Take notice that anyone caught giving information as to the shooting of the peelers at Soloheadbeg will meet with the same fate. Signed, Veritas." I then tore down the poster which the British soldiers had put up and replaced it by my own notice. I mention this incident specifically because it was later, on two occasions, the subject of parliamentary questions in the British House of Commons.'

At the inquest into the deaths of the two Soloheadbeg constables, county council worker Patrick Quinn gave some confused evidence as to what he had seen and then he collapsed in a fit. He was removed from the room. After a brief second spell in the witness box he had to be sent to hospital, suffering from a complete nervous breakdown.

The coroner said that Constable McDonnell had been in Tipperary for thirty years and a more quiet or inoffensive man he had never met. The inquest heard that McDonnell had been shot in the left side of the head and that, from the track of the bullet, he must have been in a crouching position and been fired on from behind.

As for the Big Four, as Robinson, Treacy, Hogan and Breen were now known, they took to the hills. 'We were to be outlaw raparees,' Breen said, 'with a price on our heads.' They moved fast and they moved often. They were only welcome in certain homes and districts; they could only trust certain families. A safe house was only safe for a day or two. Breen said that former friends shunned them, preferring the drawing-room to the battlefield.

Hogan, Treacy and Breen moved around together from the day of Soloheadbeg on, but Robinson returned home to Kilshenane, only later hooking up with the others. 'I went to Kilshenane to fix up contacts,' he explained, 'and to find out what the reactions were.' According to both Eamon O'Duibhir and Breen, Robinson went back to Kilshenane with the intention of resuming his bucolic life as a farm worker. O'Duibhir said that he 'tackled the work again but, after Soloheadbeg, he was no longer able to come to Kilshenane except on the quiet.' Breen said, 'Robinson was separated from us then, as he apparently had intended to carry on with his work at Ballagh with Eamon O'Dwyer.'

There is some dispute as to how long it took him to rejoin his comrades and there are signs that he had no idea where they had gone. Paddy O'Dwyer recalled that, a few days after Soloheadbeg, Robinson visited him at his Hollyford home: 'Séamus was anxious to get in touch with Treacy, Breen and Hogan.' O'Dwyer couldn't help Robinson because he had no idea of their whereabouts.

Breen claimed that it was some weeks afterwards, when someone told Robinson that he was about to be arrested in connection with Soloheadbeg, that he went on the run and joined the other three. 'In fact,' Breen maintained, 'I think it was about six weeks afterwards.' This would seem to be a wildly incorrect recollection.

Robinson had certainly joined them by the time Treacy called a meeting of brigade officers at Donnelly's of Nodstown, near Cashel, on 23 February. At that gathering, Robinson drafted the proclamation which ordered all British military and police forces to leave south Tipperary under penalty of death. It said that all upholders of the 'foreign government' found in the county after that date would be held to have forfeited their lives. GHQ refused to ratify the proclamation, pointing out that the Third Tipperary Brigade was effectively making policy on the hoof and on behalf of the entire revolutionary movement. Breen, in *My Fight for Irish Freedom*, said that, 'We could not understand their reluctance, seeing that ours was the only logical position.'

The proclamation – despite the Dublin objections – was distributed throughout the brigade area. Robinson said that it was intended to put things on a war footing.

Maurice Crowe said that: 'After Soloheadbeg I again came in contact with Seán Treacy, Dan Breen and Seán Hogan near

Galbally. We proceeded from there to Lackelly and Doon, where we again met the brigade commanding officer, Séamus Robinson, and from there we went to Croughmorka. I was then sent back to get the RIC men's rifles which were hidden near the scene of the Soloheadbeg ambush. I did this in company with Tadgh Crowe of Solohead and brought these arms to my home in Glenbane. They were in the custody of my brother, Edmund, until they were handed over some months later to Dinny Lacey of the Fourth Battalion.'

His mission completed, Crowe commenced the difficult task of linking up, once more, with the hard travelling Soloheadbeg co-conspirators: 'When we got to Doherty's, they had gone on to Kennedy's of Glengroe, at the foot of the Keeper Hill. We proceeded there but, when we got to Kennedy's at 3 a.m., they had gone to Hewitt's of Ballinahinch. We stayed at Kennedy's until the following evening and at last located the others at Hewitt's where we stayed until the next evening and proceeded mostly on foot to Castleconnell where we met Seán Connolly ... We went from there that night to the Falls of Doonass to a watchman's hut at the Turbines. Here we stayed a couple of days until a message came as a result of which Robinson and Treacy went to Dublin and Breen and Hogan to east Limerick.'

As they made their way to Dublin, Treacy and Robinson's car broke down outside Marlboro jail and several British soldiers came to their assistance, eventually getting the car going. On arrival in Dublin word was sent to GHQ that they were in town. They got a message telling them where they were to meet Michael Collins.

'Michael was waiting for us on the street with his notebook out,' said Robinson. That this meeting was to be on the street instead of in an office was the first indication Robinson had that, 'if we [the Big Four] were not exactly *persona non-grata*, at best we were decidedly not warmly welcome in any HQ office … they were rightly afraid of our blazing trail being followed by spies.'

Collins seemed to be keeping his eyes peeled, watching everyone in the street without moving his head.

'Well,' he said, 'everything is fixed up; be ready to go in a day or two.'

'To go where?' Robinson asked.

'To the States,' Collins replied.

'Why?'

'Well, isn't it the usual thing to do after …' Collins allowed his sentence to trail off.

'We don't want to go to the States or anywhere else,' Robinson insisted.

'Well,' said Collins, 'a great many people think it is the only thing to do.'

'Look here,' said Robinson, worried that Sinn Féin-style pacifism had taken hold of GHQ, 'to kill a couple of policemen for the country's sake and leave it at that by running away would be so wanton, as to approximate too closely to murder.'

'Then what do you propose to do?' asked Collins.

'Fight it out, of course.'

'Mick Collins,' Robinson said, 'without having shown the slightest emotion during this short interview, now suddenly closed his notebook with a snap, saying as he strode off with the faintest of faint smiles on his lips but with a big laugh in his eyes: "That's all right with me".'

7

GELIGNITE

Gelignite is made using a type of gun cotton dissolved in nitro-glycerine and mixed with wood pulp and sodium or potassium nitrate. Its composition makes it easily mouldable and safe to handle without protection, so long as it's not near anything that could detonate it. It is one of the cheapest of explosives, mainly used for large-scale blasting in the construction and mining industries. It burns slowly and cannot explode without a detonator. Because of this it can be stored safely. Unlike dynamite, gelignite does not suffer from the dangerous problem of sweating: the leaking of unstable nitroglycerine from the solid matrix.

The Soloheadbeg gelignite – over one hundred pounds (forty-five kilos) of it in three wooden cases – was initially hidden in a ditch by the roadside at Lisheen Grove – Treacy and Breen's old meeting place – and covered with leaves. They dumped the horse and cart elsewhere, and scattered a few sticks of gelignite nearby as a decoy.

From the Tuesday of the ambush until the following Friday – 24 January – the boxes were left untouched. A small team of local Volunteers and Cumann na mBan women observed and guarded the concealed booty from a distance. Larry Power from Donohill and Norah O'Keefe, Breen and Treacy's good friend, organised this.

On one occasion a military truck drove right up to the hiding spot and broke down. This false alarm led to the decision to move the explosives somewhere less vulnerable. On the Friday night, Tom Carew (subsequently intelligence officer of the Third Tipperary Brigade) and his brother approached the explosives dump driving a cart loaded with timber. The brothers put the three cases on the driver's seat, covering them with an overcoat. Carew then lit his pipe and drove off at a leisurely pace. As they moved away from the Grove several military vehicles passed them, stopping Carew because he had no lights on his cart. He told them there was no need for lights as there was a full moon.

Carew then hid the consignment – covered with hay – in a mangold pit on his farm at Golden Garden, near Cashel, until a more secure hiding place could be dug on a part of his land where cattle foddered. All soil and sand was removed from the pit and thrown into a nearby stream. The boxes were then inserted into the hole. Alternate layers of clay and stones were placed on top of them, and finally, the topsoil was replaced.

There the booty rested until, one day, fourteen lorries showed up at Golden Garden. Over 200 RIC men and soldiers spread out, armed with spades, picks and long spikes. They also had meticulously detailed maps of the farm. The raid that followed went on for hours.

'When it started,' Desmond Ryan reported in *Seán Treacy and the Third Tipperary Brigade*, 'Carew was out working on the land and managed to conceal a revolver and get rid of some ammunition. As he entered the house he was placed under arrest and armed guard along with the other members of his family.'

The British forces carefully scrutinised and probed the entire farm. Carew, alert to the fact that he had probably been the victim of a well placed informer, could hear excited shouting going on all around the farmhouse.

Eventually, down by the stream, a shrill whistle was blown and there was animated yelling. Virtually every one of the searchers dashed to the scene, leaving only a handful of men to guard the Carew family. 'On the very spot where the dump had been sunk,' wrote Ryan, 'the raiders were working furiously, spades, picks and spikes all in action.' The spikes were thrust deeply into the exact place where the boxes were buried. It subsequently emerged that a spike had even struck one of the boxes and broken off a splinter of wood from its lid.

Amazingly, the men failed to discover the boxes and eventually the search was called off. The gelignite rested easy at Golden Garden until the following November, by which time the tentative war which its capture initiated was getting into full swing.

Around 10 November one box was sent to the south Tipperary brigade HQ, one to the Tipperary town battalion and one to the Rosegreen district. It was first used during an attack on Drombane Hall in January 1920.

'Shortly before the Truce, what was left of the gelignite taken at Soloheadbeg was used to destroy Ballydrehid and Alleen bridges,' said Tadgh Crowe. 'Ballydrehid Bridge was blown up by the battalion staff, that is by Brian Shanahan, Arthur Barlow, James Maloney, Matt Barlow and myself. I was present too at the destruction of Alleen Bridge. That was about a week before the Truce and I may say that I felt a sense of relief at seeing the end of that gelignite. Its history and its hairbreadth escapes from recapture by the military and police after the Soloheadbeg ambush … were almost as varied and as exciting as those of any of the men who took it.'

8

THE KNOCKLONG RESCUE

The impressive thing about the rescue of Seán Hogan at Knocklong train station on the evening of Tuesday, 13 May 1919, was the manner in which the rest of the Big Four acted in instant harmony, like a hammer coming down on a nail. In *My Fight for Irish Freedom*, Breen would claim that they all felt it was 'the decree of history' that they would stand or fall together. Knocklong bears out this poignant contention.

On Sunday, 11 May, a late night dance took place at Kilshenane. Eamon O'Duibhir, the host, said that, 'the young and the brave and the beautiful from the countryside were there in great numbers. Seán O'Treasaigh, Seán Hogan, Séamus Robinson and, I think, Dan Breen were there. We were all there.'

Mick Davern (Second Tipperary Brigade and, later, a popular Fianna Fáil TD) remembered: 'Séamus, Dan, Seán and J. J. [Seán Hogan] and about seventy or eighty couples attended the dance which was under a heavy guard and covered by excellent scouting. The dance continued without incident until 5 a.m. … I had been keeping company with Mary O'Brien of Rossmore who was a prominent Cumann na mBan girl for some years and Seán Hogan was in love with Bridie O'Keefe of Glenough. Hogan intimated to me that he was returning with me to Rossmore. I informed Seán Treacy, who warned me, "Don't leave him out of your sight and I will wait for ye at Lacey's Cross", which was near Glenough. I pumped Hogan's bike and the four of us proceeded towards the village of Ballagh. When we got there Hogan asked me for the pump again, I handed it to him; he put it his pocket and said, "Tell the boys I'll be in Glenough about four this evening". I argued with him and told him of my promise to Seán Treacy and tried to get hold of his bike, but he jumped on it shouting, "Two is company, three is a crowd".'

For the first time in his life Davern dreaded his next meeting with Treacy, where he would have to explain what had happened. When they met, Treacy, known for his even temper, was visibly exasperated. He said he would have disciplinary action taken against Hogan and fumed that this was not Hogan's first breach of authority. 'This is not your fault, Mick,' he said to Davern. 'and this is not the first time he did such things. I will teach him sense when I get hold of him.'

On 12 May, Hogan was advised, as he breakfasted and relaxed in the farmhouse where he'd stayed overnight, that there was about to be a raid. A party of RIC was approaching with the intention of making a low-key inspection of the farmhouse, as opposed to hunting for one of the Soloheadbeg gang.

Hogan proceeded to walk directly into, instead of escaping from, the search party. His friends attributed his arrest to his unfamiliarity with the terrain but it seems that he could easily have escaped if he'd listened to his hosts. This debacle was an example of what was kindly referred to as his lack of common sense.

At the time of his arrest, Hogan was not identified; he was really detained because he was caught trying to make an escape. Transferred to Thurles, he was interrogated there and, eventually, recognised as one of the notorious 'Soloheadbeg Murder Gang'. Security was tightened around him as plans were made to transfer him to Cork.

When Robinson, Treacy and Breen heard of Hogan's arrest and that he was in Thurles, they made an urgent decision to rescue him. In the preceding years they and their friends had been in and out of prison often so they knew all about the entire process of arrest, custody and incarceration. It was likely that Hogan would very soon be transferred – by train – to Cork. They would free him while he was in transit on that train.

Assistance of various sorts was sought and, in the meantime, they set about choosing a suitable train station at which to stage the rescue. Goold's Cross, Emly and Knocklong were considered suitably small and unguarded.

Treacy established a mission headquarters at Maloney's of Lackelly, not far from Emly. There, in the early hours of 13 May, Robinson, Breen and Treacy sat around the breakfast table and worked out a plan. Treacy fretted about which station would prove the best bet, which would be furthest from RIC and army reinforcements, and which would allow the greatest hope of a getaway. The freeing of J.J. Hogan – as everybody knew him – was due to be an all-Tipperary action, but local factors intervened.

Emly and Knocklong, being in Co. Limerick, were outside the Tipperary men's brigade area. There were friendly ties between the east Limerick and south Tipperary IRA – they regularly co-operated on important jobs – but the Galbally brigade, within whose area the rescue was to be attempted, were territorial enough. They were happy to allow the Big Three across their borders but they baulked at allowing virtual hordes of Tipperary fighters into their space.

Mick Davern from Cashel had been approached on 12 May by Patrick McCormack, one of the Soloheadbeg gang, with a verbal instruction from Séamus Robinson. Davern was to proceed immediately to mobilise twenty-five men – or as many as he could arm – and to bring them under cover to within striking distance of Goold's Cross train station. 'I carried out this order,' said Davern. 'I had them billeted in an old shed about one and a half miles from the station. Some of the men had no idea why they were there, but they were told that they would have no option but to fight in a few hours. They were quite happy and I told them that if the fight came off I had arranged for Father Matt Ryan to give them General Absolution.'

The next morning Davern was told that the plan had changed. Now the rescue would be done at Emly and, more importantly, his Tipperary men would not be needed. The Galbally battalion would supply enough men and whatever else was required.

At Lackelly, the decision was finally made to stage the rescue at Knocklong. The countryside around Knocklong was quiet and, on one side of the station, deserted. The two nearest barracks were more than three miles away.

Using an elaborate panoply of lookouts, telegrams and local Volunteers, a theoretically foolproof scheme was worked out. Women and men set about watching Thurles Barracks, train station and points in between there and Knocklong. Coded telegrams would be used to convey news of Hogan's movements.

At 1.29 p.m. the morning train from Dublin pulled into Knocklong. Hogan's pals went on board but found no sign of him. The three then returned to Lackelly and prepared to meet the evening train, due into Knocklong at 8 p.m. Five Galbally

IRA men were recruited and made their way to Lackelly where the plan was being revised.

As the Cork-bound train made its way south, four Galbally Volunteers got on board at Emly, the stop which preceded Knocklong. They soon discovered that Hogan was on the train, guarded by four armed RIC men.

They were to warn the Knocklong rescuers – Breen, Robinson, Treacy and Eamonn O'Brien, a Galbally man closely linked to the Big Four – that Hogan was there and to indicate exactly which compartment he was held in.

Hogan sat in a compartment, handcuffed and seated between Sergeant Wallace and Constable Enright. Both men carried revolvers. Opposite Hogan there were two other constables, Ring and Reilly, both bearing shotguns. Sergeant Wallace was an important political officer, his pre-eminence shown by the fact that he was in charge of a key prisoner like Hogan.

Treacy and Eamonn O'Brien walked down to Knocklong station, while Breen and Robinson entered the town on bikes. Breen and Robinson were to linger around the station entrance, acting as lookouts, while O'Brien and Treacy went in to free Hogan.

When the train pulled into the station, two of the Galbally men jumped out before it ground to a halt. One of them pointed to the compartment where Hogan sat under guard. Treacy and O'Brien strode onto the train, revolvers drawn.

They made their way to Hogan's compartment, thrust open its sliding door and shouted, 'Hands up! Come on, Seán, out!' Constable Enright placed a revolver against Hogan's neck and crouched in behind him for cover. Treacy and O'Brien opened fire, killing Enright. 'We certainly would never have fired if Enright had not made a move to attack Hogan,' O'Brien later maintained.

Hogan jumped up and crashed his handcuffed hands right into the face of Constable Ring, seated opposite him. Treacy and Wallace wrestled viciously with one another, while Eamonn O'Brien and Constable Reilly fell into a similar struggle. Then the Galbally contingent stormed onto the train virtually unarmed and wrenched Reilly's shotgun away from him. One of them smashed him across the head with his own weapon and he collapsed onto the floor, apparently knocked out. Constable Ring either jumped out a window or was thrown out through it. This was the last that was seen or heard of him for some time.

Treacy, still wrestling with Wallace, told Hogan to leave the train. The teenager withdrew, with difficulty, as far as the corridor. There were now so many people in the small compartment that chaos reigned. While the tenacious Wallace and the resolute Treacy remained locked in combat, Treacy repeatedly appealed to the powerfully built sergeant to give it up but one man was as stubborn as the other.

Wallace was now getting the upper hand in his struggle with Treacy. The two were grappling desperately for control of Wallace's Webley revolver, whose barrel was remorselessly turning in the direction of Treacy's head. Eamonn O'Brien fired at Wallace just as the policeman put a bullet through Treacy's neck.

Wallace fell back, mortally wounded. The rescue party was now in a position to get off the train. Treacy had little fight left in him. He later told a friend: 'I thought I was a dead man. I had to hold my head up with both hands, but I knew I could walk.'

As they made to leave they heard a shotgun going off. Constable Reilly had either feigned unconsciousness or was rapidly coming round. According to the *Tipperary Star*: 'when he recovered from the staggering jab he had received in the affray, he dashed out firing shots like a man entirely out of his senses. The stationmaster, amongst others, had a narrow shave from random bullets.'

Breen and Robinson rushed onto the platform. Breen fired fiercely at O'Reilly with an accuracy that forced him to withdraw, thereby taking pressure off the retreating rescuers. O'Reilly hit Breen twice during their fight, one bullet going through Breen's lung, the other injuring his arm.

While all this was going on, Robinson seems to have kept his distance. He may not have been a coward, but neither does it seem that he was much use in the heat of battle. Desmond Ryan, in his hagiographic account of the adventure, *Daring Rescue of Seán Hogan at Knocklong Station* is soothingly discreet about Robinson's input: 'Panic still reigned and it was some minutes before Robinson could discover the actual position. He saw, however, that the worst had not happened. He prepared to intervene as soon as he could with effect … A thought flashed into his mind, a curious oversight in the plans … there had been no provision against any attempt to start the train. Robinson hurried quickly to the spot where he could keep his eye and his gun on the engine driver. The next minute he saw Treacy, Breen and Hogan and knew that the rescue had indeed succeeded.'

Robinson's indecision, timidity and commitment to the rules of war – as he interpreted them – would gradually isolate him from the fighters he commanded. However, on that Knocklong platform, after fifteen minutes of grim struggle, his cohorts were probably lucky to have at least one of their number fully operational; Treacy tottered on the edge of unconsciousness, Breen was delirious with pain and Hogan was still handcuffed.

As the injured men were dragged away, Hogan rushed into a butcher's shop and shouted at the startled butcher, 'Take them off! Take them off!', as he held up his hands. The butcher's wife bolted the shop door, got a seven pound weight with a deep groove in it and told Hogan to place his hands over the centre bar of the weight. Her husband took his cleaver and, with one good belt, broke the handcuffs. Hogan was then guided out through the back door of the house and pointed in the direction of open country. He soon caught up with the others. The Big Four were reunited, having pulled off the sort of stunt from which legends are made.

Knocklong marked a turning point in the embryonic revolution. Soloheadbeg had not been popular with natural Volunteer constituencies such as the rural poor, small farmers, or the urban working-class. Many had disapproved of those particular killings on moral or religious grounds. But the Knocklong mêlée broadened the range of public opinion about the IRA. This time the policemen were killed in an apparently equitable fight. This time the IRA attackers were gravely injured. This time a photogenic hero had emerged from the whole thing.

Hogan was a good-looking boyish character popular with the many girls who came into contact with him at the various dances and social occasions he attended. He was just two days short of his eighteenth birthday. Guilty of conspiring to commit a crime which all governments deem evil and seditious – the killing of policemen – Hogan had faced almost certain execution in Cork. His liberation was the stuff of Hollywood movies, a profoundly dramatic affray witnessed, from a railway station platform, by shocked commuters and rail company employees. It had the effect of mobilising support for the IRA, of lending to them a glamorous vagabond image, and of exciting the inhabitants of Tipperary, Cork and Limerick.

'The police,' says Joost Augusteijn, 'reported that the killings at Knocklong were kindly received by the population.' Particularly, the RIC county inspector reported, 'in parts of Tipperary and Cashel districts peculiarly given to this form of showing hatred to constituted authority.'

For the people of south Tipperary, there was a price to pay. The area was declared a 'Special Military Area' with martial law imposed. The Special Military Area rule was designed to damage the local economy, to make life difficult and to discourage people with a stake in society from sympathising with, or in any way assisting, the rebels.

9

KNOCKLONG, THE AFTERMATH

One is not particular about personal appearance when there is an army at one's heels and a price of a thousand pounds on one's head.

Dan Breen, *My Fight for Irish Freedom*

Having left Knocklong, the gang headed for a nearby house where a doctor took a quick look at Breen and Treacy. Breen was thought to be so seriously injured that he might not make it. He was given some morphine and, afterwards, he and Treacy were moved by pony and trap* to the home of David Clancy at Ballylanders, Co. Tipperary. Clancy was a lieutenant in the local Volunteer company; his brother Patrick became – before he was shot dead in August 1920 – vice-commandant of the Third Tipperary Brigade. Vigorous security was provided for the fugitives by a roster of Volunteers.

Treacy seemed to make a miraculous recovery from what had initially looked like grave injuries and was soon back to his usual placid self. A sympathetic doctor named Fitzpatrick was summoned from Kilfinane to examine the injured men properly. Breen was in a deep drug-induced sleep. Treacy was in good spirits, complaining about nothing more serious than a problem with one of his teeth. The bullet which had gone through his throat, Fitzpatrick discovered, had damaged nothing important, and just missed his jugular vein and carotid arteries.

Dr Fitzpatrick recalled in 1945 the condition in which he had found Treacy: 'Seán Treacy was not complaining about the big and painful wound in his throat. Most men, myself included, would not have bothered about anything else. Yet all that worried Treacy was that loosened tooth. Treacy was the coolest man there, far cooler than I was. That was Seán Treacy!'

A couple of days after Knocklong a dispatch rider named Keane reached Mick Davern with a message from the Big Four, with news concerning their well-being. This information was sent, via Davern, to their families and friends: 'I was told to tell Eamon O'Duibhir that Séamus Robinson was not wounded, that Seán Hogan's mother was to be told that he was not wounded and that he was all right, to tell Seán Treacy's mother that Seán was slightly wounded in the neck but it was of slight consequence. He [Keane] also told me that they needed money very badly and he got some money from the acting QM [Eamon O'Duibhir]. He then gave me a covering address to forward the money to Miss Lily Finn, Rathkeale, Co. Limerick.

'I brought Keane to Eamon O'Duibhir's, where we ascertained that there was only £7.10 in brigade funds. I urged Eamon to give it but he replied: "What in the name of God is £7.10 to four men on the run? Tell the boys that we will go out through the companies and collect more money. We'll get Paddy Ryan [Lacken] and Paddy Kinnane to collect in the mid-Tipperary Brigade also." I proceeded to Alice Ryan of Church Street, Tipperary, a prominent Cumann na mBan girl and I met Commandant Seán Duffy of the Fourth Battalion, who was later killed. I also saw Con Moloney, acting brigade adjutant, and I informed him what had happened at Knocklong and told him to inform Mrs Treacy, Mrs Breen and Mrs Hogan. They suggested that I should go back home by Mrs Breen's, which I did. When I informed her of what had happened and that two of the RIC were killed, she said, "Oh, Christ, isn't it a pity that they didn't kill the four bastards?" The following day we collected over £100 and forwarded it. While collecting the money, we made no secret of what it was wanted for; it was for the gallant men who had rescued Seán Hogan. Some of the people who had no money in the house borrowed it from neighbours and only one man refused.'

It was vital to transfer the Big Four, to get them away from the vicinity of Knocklong. Arrangements for this removal were made by Seán Finn, the west Limerick commandant. At midnight, a few days after the rescue, two cars drove up to David Clancy's place. A weak and semi-conscious Breen was carried to one car, with Seán Hogan accompanying him. The cars moved away in convoy, one decoy car with lights full on going first while the second – carrying Hogan and Breen – followed behind in darkness.

Joost Augusteijn says that: 'The Big Four left the county to recuperate in safety. They travelled throughout the south-west and ultimately ended in Dublin, where they remained until the beginning of 1920. During their absence some of the other officers kept the organisation going, but militarily nothing happened.'

Over the summer the Big Four disappeared into the landscape. They spent time in Kerry, Cork, Clare and north Tipperary. Their absence from their south-east Tipperary strongholds caused a certain slow-down in revolutionary activities there.

Life became tricky for low-level Volunteers. The government was gradually adopting a get-tough stance in Tipperary.

The killing of Detective Inspector I. Hunt in Thurles on 23 June finally spurred Lord Lieutenant French into action. On 26 June, he telegraphed the British cabinet: 'The Irish government are now forced to conclude that Sinn Féiners in this district are an organised club for the murder of police and that the time has come when Sinn Féin and its organisation in this district of Tipperary must be proclaimed an illegal organisation.' An order proscribing Sinn Féin (plus the Volunteers, Cumann na mBan and the Gaelic League) in Tipperary North and South Riding was issued on 4 July.

In September, four Galbally men were arrested for killing the two Knocklong RIC men. Eventually two of them, Patrick Maher and Ned Foley, were charged and found guilty. They were hanged on 7 June 1921. Ned Foley *had* been part of the team which freed Hogan, but it is more or less definite that Maher played no part in the exercise. They remained buried in the grounds of Mountjoy Prison, their lot unresolved until the twenty-first century, when their remains were removed from Mountjoy and reinterred in their native place. Theirs were the last executions to take place before the Truce came into effect just one month later.

Having rested up and regained their health under the watchful eye of Clare IRA boss Mick Brennan, the Big Four decided to transfer operations to Dublin. Word of their exploits had spread far and wide and they were now revolutionary celebrities and inflammatory presences. Wherever they went, trouble for the British soon followed.

Their journey towards Dublin first took them to north Tipperary, where Nenagh's Seán Gaynor, the local IRA leader, got the job of looking after them: 'Frank McGrath made the arrangements for their transfer from Clare in a motor-car, owned and driven by Benny Gill, Nenagh. On the outskirts of Nenagh they were transferred to a post-car (a horse and side-car) owned by Frank Flannery and were driven towards Toomevara where Jim Devany ... and myself met them at Ballincrotty. We were naturally thrilled to meet such famous men and when they got off the car we could see they were provided with a small arsenal.

'Each of the four carried two revolvers and they also had a box of grenades. We took them on to Whelans of Clash and all billeting arrangements and guards were made by the Toomevara Company. They remained in the district for a week and as they were then anxious to get to Dublin via Offaly, I made arrangements for an escort and went with them to Carrigahorry, where they spent a few days.

'It is significant that the first attacks on the British in our area were made in the localities in which they billeted. Shortly after their departure a policeman was shot dead in Toomevara.'

The move to Dublin marked the end of the first phase of Breen and Treacy's exploits. Neither of them would ever settle back into Tipperary again. Such was their reputation and notoriety that they could no longer move freely around their home turf. Their presence in the countryside and the need to protect them put undue pressure on both the IRA and their followers.

This problem would be addressed in 1920 when the conflict moved on to its next stage; the flying columns were formed to deal with the fact that the most daring and pre-eminent

Volunteers could no longer live in their own communities or work within the rigid pseudo-military structure favoured by GHQ.

10

THE BIG FOUR HEAD TO DUBLIN

His enemies suggested that after the Big Four moved to Dublin sometime in the summer of 1919, Dan Breen grew addicted to the bright city lights. Some thought it was easier said than done to drag him back to Tipperary, that a venal side of his personality had emerged. He entered the city as a star of sorts and he *did* enjoy that status. He developed a taste for gambling, drinking and hanging out in establishments of dubious repute. There was no reason why he should not have taken to city living and the amount of time he spent there caused no let up in his military and political activities.

Shortly after the Big Four arrived in town Breen had a some-what edgy meeting with Richard Mulcahy, who clearly did not want this Tipperary team in Dublin. Not for the first time, it was suggested that all four should disappear into America.

'Mulcahy advanced a certain line of argument as to why we should allow ourselves to be smuggled away to America,' said Breen. 'We told him against that, that we had no intention of leaving the country, to which he replied that, if we persisted in staying here, we would be disobeying the ruling of the general staff. He pointed out that the general staff could not allow itself to be pushed into war before it was ready to take such action itself and that our action at Soloheadbeg and Knocklong, having been taken entirely on our own responsibility, could not be stood over by GHQ. He said that, if we insisted on staying in the country and if we were arrested or killed by the enemy, GHQ could not acknowledge us as acting with authority and that we would, therefore, be branded as murderers. I said that we realised all that, but that we still intended to stay here and to carry on the fight we had begun, following which Mulcahy then made the extraordinary suggestion that, if we persisted in remaining, GHQ had authorised him to offer us a payment of £5 a week to keep us. To this offer I replied that, if we were to be considered as murderers, at least we would not justify the name of paid murderers and that our friends, who had been so kind as to keep us all this time, would no doubt continue to do so.'

Mulcahy soon had to bow to the will of others – Collins wanted the Big Four around – but at the end of his life he was still telling his son that events like Soloheadbeg had, 'pushed rather turbulent spirits such as Breen and Treacy into the Dublin arena from time to time where their services were not required and their presence was often awkward.'

'Turbulent spirits' were exactly what Collins wanted for what became known as the Squad or the Twelve Apostles. This urban flying column, principally made up of working-class Dublin Volunteers, came under the control of Collins' intelligence department. The Squad's job was a specific one. They specialised in the execution of British intelligence agents and policemen who were particular diligent or arrogant in their dealings with the IRA. Mick McDonnell was their first leader, with Paddy Daly as his second-in-command; Daly later eclipsed McDonnell.

According to Joe Leonard, a close associate of Collins and

one of the most active members of the Squad, this counter-intelligence cell started in September 1919 when Mulcahy summoned a number of first-rate Volunteers to a meeting at Parnell Square, Dublin. The IRA leadership was represented by Collins, Dick McKee (commandant, Dublin Brigade), Peadar Clancy (vice-commandant, Dublin Brigade) and Mick McDonnell.

Mulcahy, said Leonard, explained that the purpose of the meeting was to tell the men of the urgent need for vigorous action 'against the British executive and political detectives who were harassing Dáil Éireann and our headquarters staff.'

The founding members of the Squad at this meeting were asked if they were prepared to give their entire time and thought to this new job. Joe Leonard thought that the men present in Parnell Square were himself, Seán Doyle, Paddy Daly, Ben Barrett and, 'the four Tipperary men from the Knocklong job, Seán Treacy, Dan Breen, J. J. Hogan and Séamus Robinson to be attached for a time.'

'While we were in Dublin,' said Breen. 'We placed ourselves at the disposal of the GHQ Squad, under Mick McDonnell at the time and there were at least four or five occasions when arrangements were made to ambush the lord lieutenant, Lord French, in all of which he failed to turn up, or in some way the arrangements proved abortive.'

According to Joe Leonard: 'It very soon became apparent that if we were to survive to carry out our work we would have to become sight invisible – with only eyes, ears, legs and hands at any particular place in daylight. All the city seemed to shrink in size and detectives grew on railings, with their attendant touts and spies.'

Breen said that: 'When I was in Dublin we lived on the

Furlongs in Drumcondra, the Bolands and some others, who not alone provided us with board and lodging but clothed us, gave us pocket money and even money to buy the arms and ammunition which we were using from time to time.'

There were many red-brick middle-class city homes – full of ardent Cumann na mBan daughters – where these dashing but violent young men were welcome. There were numerous bars and private clubs where they could safely meet up with one another. One of the things which kept dragging Breen, Hogan and Treacy back to Dublin was female company. Volunteers who'd rejected their parents' political views had no problem also rejecting their traditional social values.

One of the great 'fixers' in the Dublin of that time – Phil Shanahan – was Breen's most generous and dubious host. Shanahan – originally from Donohill – came in for fulsome praise in *My Fight for Irish Freedom*: 'We never wanted for anything when Phil was about.' A closer examination of Phil Shanahan's track record suggests exactly what this 'anything' might have been.

Shanahan owned a pub in the Monto district of Dublin, the notorious red light area down by the docks. Because he'd been involved in the 1916 Rising, he subsequently had trouble renewing his licence. He sought legal assistance from the distinguished barrister, Tim Healy, who wrote: 'I was astonished at the type of man – about forty years of age, jolly and respectable. He said he "rose out" to have a "crack at the English" and seemed not at all concerned at the question of success or failure. He was a Tipperary hurler in the old days.'

Poet and surgeon Oliver St John Gogarty suspected that Shanahan ran a brothel from his pub. In his 'Bureau of Military

History Statement' Breen at one point mentioned some people he came across: 'They said they knew me at Phil Shanahan's place in Foley Street. This was the prostitute area of Dublin.' Elsewhere he said: 'The lady prostitutes used to pinch the guns and ammunition from the Auxiliaries or Tans at night and then leave them for us at Phil Shanahan's public house. I might add that there was no such thing as payment for these transactions and any information they had they gave us.' In *My Fight for Irish Freedom* he also said that Shanahan's was 'the rendezvous of saints and sinners'.

In 1919, Breen began commuting back and forth between Dublin and Tipperary – something he did for much of the rest of his life. In later years he travelled by car. During the Tan War he made the journey any way he could: 'I'd travel by train, car, or cycle and sometimes I walked. I remember leaving Dublin one morning at 6.30 and I had a meeting in Tipperary at 6 o'clock that evening and I was the only one in time. Actually I was there ahead of time and with bad roads and carrying all my artillery too. I'd walk from Dublin to Tipperary in ten hours and fifteen or sixteen hours to make Cork from Dublin. It used to take me five days to walk to Cork across the fields.'

The absence of these enterprising young men from their homes in Tipperary hit their relatives hard. Treacy and Breen were the main providers for their respective families. Eamon O'Duibhir was summoned to Dublin in 1919 by Tom Johnson and William O'Brien from the Labour Party. Acting on behalf on the National Aid League, they offered him £200 to help meet his expenses. He turned it down but was advised by the Labour men to find out if anything useful could be done with the money back in Tipperary. He discussed it with Cumann na mBan and they pointed out that certain local families, such as Dan Breen's mother, were in a very bad way financially. National Aid gave O'Duibhir some money for these families; Mrs Breen got £80.

11

AMBUSHING LORD FRENCH

Lord John French was the King's representative in Ireland and the day-to-day ruler of the island. An army officer back from the Great War bloodbath, he gradually introduced into Ireland a succession of belligerent military methods which effectively hampered the burgeoning insurgency. Collins was determined to assassinate him on both practical and public relations grounds. There were at least twelve serious attempts to kill him and Volunteers from the country were regularly recruited for these endeavours.

Paddy O'Dwyer, one of the Soloheadbeg team, was approached by Maurice Crowe and asked if he would be prepared to go to London to take part in an attack there on French. 'He was not prepared to give me any details,' said O'Dwyer, 'nor would he disclose to me at that stage the names of any other men who were being invited to travel … This conversation with Maurice Crowe took place some months before the attack on Lord French at Ashtown.'

Frank McGrath, commandant of the north Tipperary IRA, was also sounded out: 'Some time before the attack on Lord French at Ashtown … I was called to GHQ. There I met Michael Collins, who directed me to a room in which were Cathal Brugha and Dick Mulcahy. I learned from Brugha and Mulcahy that it was proposed to make an attack on Lord French and they asked me if I was in a position to supply a number of men to assist in the operation and, if so, how many. I replied that I was confident that the men could be got but that offhand I could not give the number. I undertook that on my return home I would find out definitely and furnish the names of men agreeable to take part. This was considered satisfactory and they asked me to communicate the information within four days. No mention was made of where the proposed attack was to take place or of how the men were to be armed, but I assumed that GHQ would provide the arms. On leaving the room I met Liam Deasy from Cork, who was evidently required on a similar mission to mine, for Michael Collins sent him into the room I had just left.

'On my return home, I interviewed members of the brigade and, as a result, I sent forward to GHQ a list of some fifty names (including my own) of men who were prepared to take part in such an engagement at any time.'

It seems that GHQ favoured country men for a job which, in all likelihood, would have to be done in Dublin. Being the King's plenipotentiary in a territory more or less at war, French was heavily guarded wherever he went. In Dublin, however, he performed a number of semi-public ceremonial duties necessary to maintain the 'business as usual' stance favoured by the British.

The several Dublin attempts to eliminate him fell within the remit of the Squad and members of the Big Four were normally involved. Dan Breen said that: 'We all arranged to stay somewhere that we could be easily reached by phone, but Robinson, who was staying in Heytesbury Street, could not be contacted by phone. So I went on one of these occasions to warn him of a proposed attack, but he informed me that he was having nothing to do with it and that he was not taking part in any more of these Dublin exploits. I told Treacy about this and actually we did get him to come with us to Ashtown when the actual attack on French took place but from this on Robinson was no longer proving amenable and, on quite a number of occasions after this, he upset the applecart rather badly by giving countermanding orders when we had something arranged in Tipperary.'

One of the abortive attempts to catch French involved a plan to ambush his car as it crossed over Grattan Bridge from the viceregal lodge in the Phoenix Park, en route to an armistice banquet at Trinity College on 11 November 1919.

Seán Hogan was told the exact time that French's car was due to pass by his vantage point near Dublin Castle. At that specified time on an icy cold night Hogan pulled the pins out of the two grenades he'd been given and threw the pins away. French never showed up and Hogan ended up walking through a crowded city centre nervously bearing a live grenade in each hand, his freezing fingers anxiously clutching the grenade's taut springs.

The Ashtown attack had, of necessity, to be organised at short notice. Squad member Vinnie Byrne was socialising on the night of 18 December 1919, when he heard, via the son of a train guard, that Lord French was due to travel up to Dublin from Frenchpark, his Co. Roscommon home, the following morning. Byrne asked his companion what time his father – who was working on French's train –would get back to Dublin and the son told Byrne that the father would be home around eleven or twelve o'clock.

Being a prime target, French's movements had been diligently noted and it was known that he would disembark from his train at Ashtown Station, near his Phoenix Park residence.

'I immediately went to Mick McDonnell's house, which was in Richmond Crescent and reported to him what I had heard,' said Byrne. 'Mick said: "That's the best bit of news I've had for a long time." The next thing he said was: "You had better be here in the morning at about ten o'clock, as we might have a go at French." As it was getting late, I said to him: "I had better be off. I will see you in the morning, please God."

'The following morning I reported to Mick McDonnell on time. There was a group of men in the front room of his house and, as I went in, Mick said: "Byrne, you had better go up to the dump and bring down any grenades that are there".'

When Byrne came back with the grenades they were distributed to some of the men. Byrne was then told exactly who was present. He already knew Martin Savage (a handsome young Sligo man who'd been in the GPO in 1916), Tom Keogh (an expert marksman), Paddy Daly and Joe Leonard. McDonnell introduced him to the others in the room: Breen, Robinson, Treacy and Hogan. The would-be assasins headed off in the direction of Ashtown.

Byrne continued: 'We halted at Kelly's pub. Mick McDonnell, Dan Breen, Seán Treacy and Paddy Daly stood in a group and were having a conversation together. After a few minutes we all went into the pub. Minerals, as far as I remember, were ordered. When I had finished my glass, Mick called me and told me to get my bike, cycle towards the station and see if there was any sign of the train, or if there were any military or police there ... I had only gone about two hundred yards when I heard the sound of motor cars behind me. A motor horn sounded and I pulled into the side and let them pass. There were four cars in all. I wheeled round, cycled back as hard as I could and reported to Mick McDonnell about the military passing me going to the station.'

They began, at that moment, to hear French's train approaching. Daly, Leonard, Robinson, Treacy and Hogan went to the back yard of the pub, making their way into a field where they took up positions behind a hedge which looked out over the station road.

McDonnell, Breen and Keogh commandeered a large farm cart in the yard and attempted to move it out onto the road. The cart proved heavier than expected and it got stuck. At this moment two traffic police showed up on foot, heading in the direction of the station. The ambushers scarcely had time to register their presence when they heard the convoy of cars coming from the station. Before they knew it, French and his protectors were drawing perilously near.

'As the cars approached, the men behind the hedge opened fire with revolvers and grenades,' Byrne said. 'The first car to come was a dark blue one. Sitting beside the driver was a man in civilian clothes who, we learned afterwards, was Detective Officer Nalley. He was firing from a revolver. As the car came clear of the corner, I let fly a grenade which hit the back of the car and exploded. The next thing I saw was the peeler being blown across the road. The second car was stopped right opposite to our men behind the hedge. This car was a closed one – khaki-green in colour. The third car was a box Ford type, with a canvas roof, which flew by with a continuous fire on it. The fourth car which came along was an open Sunbeam car and in it were a soldier driver and a sergeant. The sergeant was lying across the back of the car and firing from a rifle. Where we were standing we were an open target for him. In fact you could hear the bullets whistling by, finding a billet in the wall behind us. As this car was disappearing around the wide bend of the road leading to the Ashtown Gate of the Phoenix Park, I heard Martin Savage saying something and it sounded like this: "Oh, lads, I am hit". The next moment he was dead, lying on the road.'

Breen's leg had been injured and he was bleeding copiously. The driver of the khaki-green car climbed out of his vehicle waving a handkerchief. McDonnell accepted his surrender and asked him where Lord French was. The soldier – Corporal Appleby – said that the lord lieutenant had been blown to pieces in his car. Appleby's false information was accepted, in the heat of battle, at face value. In reality, French got away unscathed. Some of the ambushers wanted to shoot Appleby but McDonnell decided to let him go.

'As we had only bicycles, we could not get Martin Savage's dead body away,' said Byrne. 'The next thing is we were told to get back into town and to travel in twos. I was about to get away when I was told to act rearguard action to Dan Breen who, after mounting his bicycle, had to lean on Paddy Daly's shoulder … We travelled along until we came to the Cabra Road and proceeded down as far as St Peter's church, Phibsboro, where we turned to the left, then to the right and along down Connaught Street on to the Phibsboro Road.

'At this time, I was cycling near Paddy Daly and Dan Breen. Paddy said to me: "You carry on Vinnie. We are all right now, I'll look after Dan" … Needless to say, on the night of the attack, I called over to Mick McDonnell's and met Tom Keogh there.

The whole conversation was about the loss of poor Martin Savage and having to leave him behind us. Perhaps while on this subject, it might be well to mention that Martin Savage was a grocer's assistant, working in Kerr's of the North Strand. On the morning of the ambush, he left the shop to bank some money for his employer. Instead of going to the bank, he came out to the job. It was, I believe, stated in the newspapers that a large sum of money was found in his possession.'

Paddy Daly, who during the Civil War played a critical part in the defeat of the anti-Treaty forces, eventually became something of a republican *bête noir*. There were Civil War stories – perhaps apocryphal – about Daly mistreating republican prisoners, man-handling women, and indulging in conduct unbecoming of an officer. Although Daly clearly helped save Breen after the Ashtown ambush, Breen eventually disapproved of him: 'While I have no time for Daly, he stood by me. I was all blood, staggering on foot and they pushed me along. I tied the leg of my trousers to hide the blood and I tried to cover my head, which was also bleeding … The most dastardly thing against Daly and Dick Mulcahy was the unfortunate boy they led to the gallows in 1924. They told this boy that his trial was only a farce and that they would get him away out of the country. This boy was tried and convicted and put into his "condemned" cell. He remarked, "I will be off to America in a few days" and it was only the day before his execution he realised it was serious. When going out to his execution he said, "There will be two men, Mulcahy and Paddy Daly, pleased that I am dancing on the trap door this morning". Kevin O'Higgins* was insisting on trials at this time.'

After Ashtown, French tended to spend most of his time in his viceregal lodge. His assailants hadn't killed him but they had

– literally – confined him to barracks. They'd scored a political point. Ireland was supposed to be a regular part of the British state, but from then on the King's man in Dublin couldn't come and go as he pleased.

The intimacy of the Dublin radical scene was illustrated, the year after Ashtown, by a chance encounter between Breen and two of the city's finest revolutionary women; he ran into Maude Gonne MacBride, the most flamboyant of the Irish activist women, and her then live-in constant companion, Charlotte Despard. Mrs Despard, an ardent feminist and socialist, was one of those somewhat eccentric upper-class protestant women who, from time to time, attached themselves to the Irish 'cause'. She was also Lord French's sister.

'I met Mrs Despard and Mrs MacBride in O'Connell Street in 1920,' said Breen. 'Mrs Despard was very annoyed with me for attacking her brother, John. But I said the only thing I was sorry for was that we did not get him. She said he was a good Irishman; but I did not discuss that with her. "Poor John dead!" said she.'

Attacks on Barracks

By 1920, the conflict between the IRA and the British government was turning nasty and bloody on both sides. In October, the
British home secretary informed the House of Commons that
between January 1919 and October 1920, 64 Irish courthouses
had been destroyed along with 492 abandoned RIC barracks,
21 occupied barracks and 148 private residences belonging to
citizens loyal to the crown. A further 114 RIC barracks had
been damaged; there had been 741 raids on the mail; 40 raids
on coastguard stations and lighthouses; 117 policemen and 23
soldiers had been killed; 185 policemen and 71 soldiers had
been wounded; 32 civilians had been killed and 83 wounded.

The terrorising Black and Tans were introduced and major
republican figures such as Tomás MacCurtain, Terence Mac-
Swiney, Kevin Barry and Seán Treacy died. The first three deaths
evoked public sympathy and, therefore, hardened nationalist
resolve. The death of Treacy tangibly affected the conduct of the
war in Tipperary and took some of the wind out of Dan Breen's
sails.

Early in the year the moderate Dublin republican leadership,
which had sought in 1919 to curtail rogue elements like the Third
Tipperary Brigade, changed their attitude. They'd invested their
hopes in gaining recognition for Ireland at the Versailles Peace
Conference, naively believing that the ostensibly self-evident

justice of their cause would be recognised by the embryonic 'International Community'. When this improbable strategy failed and when IRA activists in Cork and Dublin began to follow Tipperary's lead, GHQ dedicated itself to an armed struggle. For the rest of the Tan War, however, they sought to turn the IRA on and off like water coming out of a tap. The conflict between the Dublin-based revolutionaries' exclusively political aspirations and the IRA's more rugged approach to self-emancipation remained unresolved until Ireland endured a Civil War and witnessed the emergence of Fianna Fáil.

In 1920, regional IRA leaders came together for important jobs and, encouraged by GHQ, got to know one another. Meda Ryan found that Cork IRA leader Liam Lynch, in Dublin for a few months early in that year, was in continuous contact with GHQ staff like Collins and Mulcahy. While in town he also met up with Breen and Treacy. With them he discussed plans for developing the war and, says Ryan, they concluded there was no turning back at that stage: 'Liam's most frequent contacts were with Cork No. 1 and Tipperary No. 3 brigades which bordered his own area. Dan Breen, Seán Treacy and Denis Lacey visited him a number of times. A visit by Dan Breen towards the end of 1920 resulted in an informal conference to discuss the general situation … They sent their recommendations and a summary of their decisions to GHQ.'

The major IRA development of 1920 – the emergence of well organised attacks on RIC barracks – took on board this new spirit of inter-brigade collaboration. These fights were often sanctioned by GHQ and were usually led and planned by enthusiastic GHQ fighter-organisers like Ernie O'Malley or Thomas Malone (also known by his revolutionary political name, Seán Forde).

The plethora of copycat mini-Soloheadbegs happening all over the country had resulted in the closure of numerous minor RIC outposts, often no more than two-room cottages in isolated communities. RIC strength was now concentrated inside proper barracks, sometimes semi-fortified structures which held large numbers of men and were less easy to attack. These fortresses might house RIC, Black and Tan, British army and intelligence members.

An RIC rookie stationed in Waterford in 1920 recalled: 'We were basically looking for the IRA. No still of poteen, no light on your bike, no tail lamp, no anything, nobody bothered. The police didn't bother.' He was given one very basic piece of advice by his new colleagues: 'First take cover. Take cover and shoot after.'

Tipperary Volunteers were among the first to mount barracks' attacks and they were the most enthusiastic of attackers. In other regions, men were nervous about confronting, directly, heavily armed and protected buildings.

'A pattern to these attacks was soon established,' Joost Augusteijn said of the evolving Tipperary situation. 'The local brigade officer, together with the local battalion commandant and Ernie O'Malley, a GHQ organiser, stood in the centre of its organisation and execution. These men, who were engaged on a full-time basis in Volunteer work, were aided by the most active Volunteers of surrounding battalions. Some local companies were involved in manning blockades on the roads leading to the barracks and in dispatch riding. Those involved in the attack took up positions around the barracks, while the main assault was centred on the roof in an attempt to set the barracks alight.'

On 28 April, Ballylanders barracks was attacked. On 10

May, Hollyford barracks was besieged by Tadgh Dwyer, Séamus Robinson and Seán Treacy; Robinson took a notable part in this action. The barracks at Kilmallock, Co. Limerick – a British intelligence hub in the Tipperary/Limerick border area – was burned down on 27 May. On 3 June, Drangan barracks, after a long battle involving O'Malley, Breen, Treacy and Robinson, surrendered to the IRA.

It was during these operations that the Soloheadbeg gelignite proved useful, as did rural ingenuity. 'We had already experimented at Davins' in Rosegreen with a dauby yellow clay which would adhere in a sloping or even to an upright surface when hurled,' Ernie O'Malley wrote in *Raids and Rallies*. 'Then we had tried this clay by wrapping it around a half-stick of gelignite with a detonator and fuse attached. When its fuse was ignited and the clay thrown, the attached glutinous material adhered to the roofs of deserted outhouses on which we had tried its force. As a result of the explosions, slates were blown from a large portion of roof. This solved one problem, that of making holes in a roof at a distance from the thrower. Through the holes, grenades would be lobbed and liquid or flaming paraffin thrust directly downwards into a room. In addition the mud bombs could be used against lorries or armoured cars, for with the use of a short fuse they could be exploded quickly. They could, therefore, be employed against the reinforcements in the early morning after an attack.'

The 27 May burning on Kilmallock barracks was a major overnight operation involving IRA men from east Clare, Cork, Tipperary and Limerick. The interesting thing about this action – the ultimate example of co-operation between brigades – was that many of those who attended, who travelled long distances to be there, came to watch and to learn how such an attack could be done. Thomas Malone said that the IRA had eighty men arranged at vantage points around the barracks. Among them were key people from neighbouring brigades like Treacy, Breen and Mick Brennan from Clare. According to Malone, they were 'all anxious to see how it was done'.

East Limerick Volunteer, J. M. McCarthy, was put in charge of one of the distinguished visitors, Clare warlord, Mick Brennan: 'How he came to be present at Kilmallock I do not know, but when we were assembling to open the attack he was on the spot and I was asked to include him in my section ... I treated him as an ordinary Volunteer, to which unaccustomed role he readily adapted himself, apart from a tendency to be prolific in suggesting alternative courses of action.'

'We had very elaborate plans in connection with the attack which provided for widespread activities in the surrounding area, including north Cork, mid Limerick, south Tipperary,' noted Malone. 'The local Volunteer companies all engaged in connection with the blocking of roads and the cutting of railway lines, because we guessed that it would take a good while to capture the barracks and that enemy reinforcements might be rushed to its relief. It was, I think, actually the biggest barracks attack that took place during the whole fighting in order of importance ... I don't think anyone ever found out how many there were there in all. There were some Tans there, whose names were never given nor whose presence was ever admitted and the names of some of the people who were killed there were never published. It was our first experience of meeting the Tans. It was the first time they had been seen around there.'

Kilmallock firmly established the pattern which was followed in subsequent attacks. A hole was made in the barracks roof and petrol was poured into it. The building was burned down but the RIC never surrendered. Instead they withdrew to an outhouse and kept on fighting. Three men died at Kilmallock: two RIC members and one IRA.

Brennan from Clare clearly didn't learn all that he needed to know because, a few days later, he sought Tipperary assistance when he was planning his own barracks' assault. Ernie O'Malley was busy masterminding the Drangan attack when Brennan sent for him. 'A dispatch rider came to the back of our house,' O'Malley wrote. 'He brought us news from Mick Brennan who was brigadier of east Clare. With him, Breen, Treacy and Robinson had stayed for a while the previous year when they were being carefully sought by the British. There was to be an attack on Six Mile Bridge barracks. But Brennan needed a few men who had experience in the use of explosives to help him. Séamus Robinson and I decided that we would go on to Co. Clare and that Seán Treacy would make the necessary preliminary arrangements for the attack on Drangan with Tom Donovan.' Donovan was the commandant of the Drangan brigade.

The seven-hour fight which took place in Drangan followed the Kilmallock pattern. All roads leading into the village were blockaded and patrolled. Telegraph wires were cut. Volunteers occupied a house left unguarded by the police which was attached to one of the gables of the barracks. Treacy, Breen and Tom Donovan made mud bombs – a petrol pump and hosepipe was requisitioned in Cashel.

By 11.30 p.m. the barracks was surrounded and a relentless battle commenced. The RIC let off flares – their only means of letting the outside world know that they were beleaguered. All the while petrol was being poured onto the barracks and, eventually, it caught fire. When ammunition inside the building began to explode the RIC hoisted a white flag and surrendered.

On 21 July, an attack on Clerihan RIC barracks was called off at the last minute. Jerome Davin was one of the organisers: 'I considered that the capture of the barracks itself was as easy as cracking a nutshell. Our main concern was to hold off the British troops if they came … thus it was that the intensive blocking of the roads and the manning of the road blocks was so important. On the appointed night we went to Clerihan just after dark. Every detail was fully organised. We had a pump capable of pumping oil and petrol up to a distance of 60 yards. A load of yellow clay was brought in a horse's cart, as we intended to make the mud bombs as we required them. Milk churns were used as containers for the paraffin oil. The riflemen and shotgunmen actually went into positions around the barracks. Treacy and I then made a final check-up. Seán had a look at the barracks and at the house which I had decided we should occupy. He agreed that it was suitable as our key point of attack. It was at this point that Séamus Robinson, the brigade O/C, arrived on the scene. He had just returned from Dublin. We told him everything was ready to go ahead with the attack. He told us that, in view of a recent GHQ order, plans for major engagements, including attacks on barracks, would first have to be submitted to GHQ for sanction. There was no alternative but to call off the attack. He was very definite that this GHQ instruction should not be broken. Some of the officers present, including Ned O'Reilly and myself, were sorely disappointed, but Seán Treacy, in his cool, calm manner, gave us an example in discipline. He simply remarked: "All right Séamus, you are the boss". Treacy and I then went to a position at the door of a public house, from where we covered the door of the barracks. We were both armed with long parabellum revolvers and we feared that the police might make a sortie out of the barracks whilst our men were being withdrawn, especially as we had learned that there was a British officer in the barracks that night. While we were there we saw an RIC man who had left the public house by a rear entrance crossing a wall into the barracks yard. Seán had him covered and I remarked that he had been in the pub for a pint and that he was harmless. This remark of mine must have been overheard by someone who knew me and who did not know Treacy, for later when this particular RIC man was stationed in Lisronagh he got in touch with me and thanked me for saving his life, saying that he understood that the strange man would have shot him when he was crossing the wall had it not been for my intervention. He also gave me some useful information from time to time afterwards. To finish with Clerihan, we had a bloodless victory, for the barracks was evacuated next day and we then destroyed it to prevent its reoccupation.'

The enthusiasm of Volunteers for attacking barracks took many forms and some IRA men were inebriated by more than the love of freedom, as Breen discovered when involved in an attempt to overrun Tipperary barracks: 'They asked me to take charge of some men on the north side of the town. We had to move from three or four miles outside the town. At that time, when you made a big attack you would call all the local Volunteers. We came along near Soloheadbeg and there was a fellow called Dinny Leahy, a fireman in the local creamery. On a Saturday night, when the locals got a few bob, they'd go into the town and have their few pints of stout and Dinny, like the others, returned home this night but he was "magalore" [very drunk]. So we called out: "Din! Din!" but not a word, he was in a state of coma. The only answer we got was a semi-conscious grunt. "Come on, Din. You must get up! You are to block the roads!" Din, being now awake, exclaimed with the utmost feeling and sincerity, "I wish to Jesus Christ Ireland was free!'"

13

THE NOOSE TIGHTENS: FERNSIDE AND THE
DEATH OF SEÁN TREACY

In Templemore, a teenage republican called Jimmy Welsh got a message from the Blessed Virgin Mary, who said that she was upset by the ongoing violence in Ireland. Inspired by this visitation, Welsh discovered a holy well in his home and religious statues in the house started bleeding. Soon he was doing a roaring trade in the sale of relics, holy water and other manifestations of his miraculous good luck.

Up in Phil Shanahan's Monto pub, Breen – a well known sceptic when it came to all matters religious – was given the job of investigating the Templemore 'miracles': 'Collins ordered me to get in touch with this "saint" from Templemore. He was the fellow who operated the bleeding statue. I met him over in O'Neill's in Pearse Street. But we did not trust him; we thought he was a spy. I went across and Dinny Lacey was with me, also many others. I brought Dinny into O'Neill's in Pearse Street. The "saint" was in the next room and when it came to my turn to be interviewed, Dinny said: "The next time he meets the Blessed Virgin Mary, be sure to insist on nothing less than a Republic." Dinny was a very solid catholic. I said to the "saint", "How do you do, boy?" After about fifteen minutes' talk I mentioned going but he insisted on going first. They were kissing his coat. Collins said, "One can't take any notice of what you say, Breen, because you have no religion." That was the last I saw of the failure, Welsh. Phil Shanahan took a car to Templemore and brought a bottle of water back with him. He wanted me to take a drop of it, but I declined.'

In May, Seán Treacy, thinking about marrying his girlfriend, Mai Quigley, wrote whimsically to Cait de Paor, a prominent member of Tipperary Cumann na mBan, concerning the implications of marriage: 'I can't agree with your opinion that marrying amounts to becoming a passive resister. History, past and present, disproves that theory. So don't let your members off work just because they're married.'

Investigating fake miracle workers and thinking about the vagaries of married life provided light relief as the noose tightened around Breen and Treacy. They'd now been spending a lot of time in Dublin so British intelligence had familiarised itself with their look, style and activities. When the IRA successfully lured Inspector Brien, a Dublin Castle intelligence gatherer, out onto the street where they could get a good shot at him, the adversaries inadvertently ended up talking to one another face-to-face in the rain while Liam Tobin, Collins' trusted intelligence chief, looked on in horror. Breen said: 'Neither of us knew Brien, so we had to go to Tobin at Vaughan's Hotel, Parnell Square and ask him to come and identify Brien. We did get Tobin and we went ahead, it being arranged that Tobin would come along and join us. We set off about 8.20. It was pouring rain. We stood in the archway at the Mail Office and this powerful man came along. He said he thought he'd wait until the rain stopped. No sign of Brien or Tobin coming! We were there until about 8.40. There were some fellows on the other side of the street. The big man said, "I don't think it will clear at all. I'll be off." The fellows across the street moved off too. Up came Tobin. "What kept you?" we asked. "Weren't ye talking to him for the last fifteen minutes?" said Tobin. But he was evidently covered by the boys on the other side of the street.'

Having spent the summer of 1920 in Tipperary participating in barracks attacks, Breen came back to Dublin in August: 'Collins notified me to come back. I had been down the country for some time. Then we had some scraps in Dublin but these were not much. In one scrap, when I remained in bed, Treacy got the sole shot off his shoe. This was in Beresford Place. Some fellow was coming in from Belfast; they went down to get him, but without success.'

On the night of 11 October, Treacy and Breen were cornered in Fernside, a middle-class Dublin safe-house in Drumcondra belonging to Professor Carolan from the nearby teacher training college. This bloody encounter resulted in Breen – after a hair-raising escape which involved face-to-face shoot outs, leaps from first floor windows, and rearguard shooting as he disappeared through adjacent back gardens – being secretly moved to the Mater Hospital by Squad members including Joe Leonard and Dick McKee. Professor Carolan died later in hospital from his injuries. Desmond Ryan quoted a British officer as saying that five British soldiers were killed.

The British fatalities at Fernside included Major George Smyth. Smyth's brother, Colonel Brice-Ferguson Smyth, RIC divisional commander for Munster, had been slain in Cork the previous July. Smyth's other brother had been killed in Lisburn.

Dan Breen later told of his injuries: 'When we got out

through the window we continued out through the back and over the walls down by St Patrick's Training College. I was not wearing boots because I was caught in bed and I broke my toes. I went on towards Glasnevin after that … The first shot fired wounded my right hand and then I had to use my left hand. I had many wounds, including leg wounds. At the time I was more or less oblivious to my wounds, but I suffered great pain afterwards.'

Eamon O'Duibhir's sister, Mrs Duncan, lived in Stella Gardens, Irishtown and her home was a safe house regularly used by Collins and the Big Four. 'I have always felt that had Breen and Treacy got to me in Stella Gardens in the week before the battle at Carolan's,' O'Duibhir said, 'the Duncans and I would have got them shelter in that working-class district. It is known that they were hard-pressed to get shelter in the city.'

Breen, despite the showy style of *My Fight for Irish Freedom*, was not especially given to self-importance but he did feel that the Fernside ambush was a direct attempt by Smyth to kill him. Incorrect rumour had it that Breen had killed his brother in Cork and Breen felt Smyth had been seeking revenge: 'Colonel Smyth was in India and he brought eleven picked men over here with him to avenge the shooting of his brother or brothers. They didn't know Treacy was there. They thought it was Lacey was with me. When Smyth heard that I had gone into a house in Drumcondra, he called his "braves" and decided to go down and get me and to bring me back and skin me alive. Smyth was cautioned to look out for me, that "this fellow will fight", but he said, "No, they are only rats; I'll bring him back alive and I'll skin him alive". And he meant it. He did not go back because he was killed and they say eleven of his pals were killed with

'The Happy Warrior'. Working on a Tipperary farm in 1921.

L to R: Seamus Robinson, Seán Hogan, Seán Treacy, Dan Breen, and Mick Brennan (Clare IRA). Seán Hogan was not present when this portrait was taken – his image was subsequently superimposed.

Members of Third Tipperary Brigade with seized cars

Cahir Flying Column

Pierce McCan   Eamonn O'Duibhir

Wedding of Dan and Brigid Malone with Seán Hogan
and Aine Malone, the bride's sister, behind.

Fr O'Leary, Breen, and Jack Sharkey at Breen's wedding. Sharkey
was the brigade's photographer.

Cumann na mBan members – Maureen, Tess and Nana Power

RIC photograph captured by IRA intelligence staff, with
information concerning individual policemen penciled in.

Breen at Leopardstown Races, circa 1928

L to R: Breen, De Valera, Robinson, John Joe O'Brien, Seán Hogan, and Ned O'Brien attending a commemoration of the Knocklong rescue.

Mick Davern, Frank Loughman, and Breen
All three were Fianna Fáil TDs in south Tipperary

Dan Breen's funeral at Donohill

POLICE NOTICE.

£1000 REWARD

WANTED FOR MURDER IN IRELAND.

DANIEL BREEN

(calls himself Commandant of the Third
Tipperary Brigade).

Age 27, 5 feet 7 inches in height, bronzed complexion, dark hair (long in front), grey eyes, short cocked nose, stout build, weight about 12 stone, clean shaven ; sulky bulldog appearance ; looks rather like a blacksmith coming from work ; wears cap pulled well down over face.

him. On that night in Drumcondra Treacy was with me and neither of us was in good health after being severely wounded. We had been on the move more or less since 1916 … We were just caught in a corner.'

Treacy escaped from Fernside, only to be gunned down on Talbot Street three days later. Jerome Davin had a poignant last encounter with Treacy in Tipperary shortly before the Fernside affray: 'It was at my sister's (Mrs Looby's) house that he shaved and dressed before taking his departure. That would, I'd say, be about a week before he was killed. He told me he was going to Dublin but did not say why he was going there. Before leaving Looby's he wrote his name and the date on a sheet of paper and handed it to my sister. She still has it in her scrapbook.'

A week later the news of Treacy's death reached Davin via a telegram from Michael Collins: 'Séamus Robinson asked me to go to Tipperary town to make the funeral arrangements. A large force of British troops were present at Limerick Junction when the train bringing the remains arrived, but I must say that on that particular night they certainly were not aggressive. As a matter of fact, a party of them presented arms as the coffin covered with the tricolour was borne from the train to the hearse. From Limerick Junction to the church at Solohead the route was lined with British troops, but this did not prevent hundreds of people, including many Volunteers, from marching behind the hearse. Next day when the burial took place British troops were again present in and around the cemetery at Kilfeacle, but the only action they took was to seize some bicycles which were left around by their owners. The officer withdrew the military before the grave was filled in and there was no interference with the firing party who fired the three volleys with revolvers

… To my mind Seán Treacy's death was the biggest blow the Third Tipperary Brigade could or did receive.'

'People were always telling Seán as he left their houses, "Be careful this time, Seán",' said Breen. 'His reply always was, "The other fellows better be more careful". That meant that he would fight to the end – no matter what the odds. And he did that in Talbot Street the day he was killed.'

Maurice McGrath, of the Third Tipperary Brigade, claimed: 'Some days after Seán Treacy's funeral, the Dwyer's homestead at Ballydrehid was raided about midnight by a party of armed and masked men and two brothers, Frank and Ned, were taken outside the door and shot dead, bayoneted and beaten to pulp with rifle buts in the presence of their sister, Kate, who tried to save them. She was the local captain of Cumann na mBan. The eldest brother, who was the local company captain, escaped, as his parents prevailed on him to hide beneath their bed …
… The company captain had forbidden the principal of the local school to open on the day of Seán Treacy's funeral – all schools were to be closed as a mark of respect and mourning. All schools, except Ballydrehid, obeyed the order, so the captain had the children turned back in the morning and no school was held. It was clear that this shooting of the Dwyer brothers was a reprisal, as the principal of the school was a policeman's wife.'

14

ENDING THE TAN WAR

We crossed the pleasant valleys and the hilltops green
Where we met with Dinny Lacey, Seán Hogan and Dan Breen
Seán Moylan and his gallant band they kept the flag flying high
Farewell to Tipperary said the Galtee Mountain Boy.

In 1921, the Third Tipperary Brigade both unravelled and consolidated. Dan Breen got married, Dinny Lacey emerged as a *de facto* Tipperary leader and Eamon O'Duibhir grew alienated from the war. Two flying columns absorbed the top IRA men in the county.

The myth of the Big Four disintegrated. Séamus Robinson, isolated at the brigade's new Rosegreen HQ, was now ignored by the Volunteers in the field. Seán Hogan led a flying column, but there were substantial murmurings of discontent about his stewardship. Breen became the inheritor of the Big Four's mantle. Despite huge personal setbacks, he remained a major organiser and, more importantly, a valiant source of inspiration to younger Volunteers wherever he went.

The death of Seán Treacy had inadvertently brought to public attention a split which had been building up in south Tipperary for some time: a letter critical of the ongoing campaign, written by Eamon O'Duibhir, was found in Treacy's pocket.

Earlier in 1920, O'Duibhir had contacted GHQ to complain

about what he saw as IRA disorder and incompetence. He was also disturbed by the organisation's failure to protect the ordinary people of Tipperary who were really suffering at the hands of the Black and Tans.

GHQ asked Robinson to investigate O'Duibhir's misgivings and Robinson reported that he found little of substance in his old mentor's complaints: 'Eamon O'Dwyer is acting brigade QM and is the best man for the job that we know. He is a man who can form opinions of his own and who will speak them when he thinks they will receive attention. I would ask GHQ to take his integrity and sincerity for granted and to ask him for a full statement of whatever case he has.'

Frank Drohan, commandant of the Clonmel battalion, became another prominent dissident. He'd been complaining since 1919 that unauthorised activities by the Big Four were 'creating disturbances'. Drohan came in for somewhat rougher treatment than O'Duibhir. In May 1921, when he tried to get selected as a candidate for the next general election, Ernie O'Malley left him in no doubt that he was considered an inappropriate nominee: 'Our point of view is that of the IRA. As an officer you are unsuitable. You had not the necessary drive and initiative for guerrilla warfare. Your area, though possessing good material, was the slackest from the point of view of organisation and offensive action. I did not nor do doubt your intentions. You are fit for civic honour but as a fighting man I do not respect you. I think that active members of the IRA are the most suitable men at present for the TD position, men whom the youth can look to for their fighting record.'

The O'Duibhir letter found on Treacy's body, in which he expressed qualms about IRA ambushes, was unsurprisingly seized upon by the British propaganda machine and published in the newspapers. When a namesake of O'Duibhir's was murdered in mysterious circumstances in Tipperary, causing speculation that the one-time Kilshenane leader (his house was now burned down) had been executed by his own side as a result of his dissension, O'Duibhir was forced to clarify his position.

In yet another letter, which appeared in the *Irish Independent* on 6 November 1920, he wrote: 'The statement contained in that letter ... alluded to my opposition to certain methods of warfare (notably ambushes) and I wish to make it clear that the only people whom I am in danger from are the agents of the British government who have already made one attempt to kill me and failing in that mission have burned down my home to ashes. In a letter of mine which appeared in the press I made the statement that I consider ambushes an unfair method of fighting. Since then the agents of the English government have perpetrated several atrocities too fresh in the public mind to need particularising. It is nearly impossible to talk of fair play in fighting such an enemy.'

The concept of the flying columns – a group of top men who kept constantly on the move and rarely returned to their homes – was Seán Treacy's parting gift to his old comrades. 'It was Treacy who first advocated setting up flying columns in Co. Tipperary,' Breen told Jim Maher. 'Shortly before his death he told me that he was thinking of returning to Tipperary to form the first flying column in the country. But he never got back to do it.'

On 4 October 1920, GHQ issued a memo calling for columns to be established throughout the country: 'At the present time a large number of both our men and officers are on the run in different parts of the country. The most effective way of using these officers and men would seem to be by organising them as flying columns. In this way – instead of being compelled to a haphazard and aimless course of action – they would become available as standing troops of a well trained and thoroughly reliable stamp and their actions would be far more systematic and effective.'

Thomas Ryan, of the Second South Tipperary Flying Column, reported: 'Almost immediately following Treacy's death the columns were formed and the whole of the best fighting men were concentrated in the operations and activities of these special units. The activities of the brigade staff from then on became almost purely administrative, giving support to the columns by intelligence and communication services. From the time the columns began Robinson remained in and about the brigade headquarters at Rosegreen, taking no active part in the work of the columns and so was not regarded by the men of the columns as having any effective control of them.'

Flying columns sometimes billeted in friendly safe houses and, just as often, slept under the stars. Tipperary No. 1 Flying Column was set up in October 1920, with rising star Dinny Lacey in command. There were approximately seventy men in his unit.

Lacey was a first cousin of Tom Carew from Golden Garden, the man who'd successfully hidden the Soloheadbeg gelignite. Lacey had been taught, like Treacy and Breen, by rebel teacher Charlie Walshe. Desmond Ryan said of Lacey's command: 'Lacey's column was to march and fight from the Tipperary border in the west to Carrick-on-Suir, over the wild expanse of country between the Comeragh Mountains, eastward from Fethard to the Kilkenny border.'

To some extent the evolution of the Tipperary columns was a response to the failure, noted by O'Duibhir, of the IRA to vigorously defend their own civilian population. 'The formation and rise of flying columns,' said Mossie McGrath from Seán Hogan's column, 'certainly put a stop to a lot of the midnight raids on Volunteer's houses and the bullying of defenceless people.'

In January 1921 – or perhaps earlier – a second, smaller, column, commanded by Hogan but overseen by Breen, was established. This contained in the region of forty men. Thomas Ryan recalled that the No. 2 Column had been established late in 1920 but he reckoned that nothing much happened with them until Dan Breen came into the area and gave them a shot in the arm: 'We knew, or rather we felt, that Breen's arrival meant that something was about to happen, that we were about to take some action, Breen's attitude being: "It's time something happened around here." We felt that his presence in the area meant that there was going to be action and we were all delighted at the prospect and to have Breen with us … On the evening of his first visit Breen came to the house of a family named Fitzgerald, about half a mile from my home. Hogan appointed me as chief scout as I knew the area well. We set off on our first march from Prendergast's to Fitzgerald's. Breen had joined us at Prendergast's and marched with us to Fitzgerald's but this was our first march openly as an armed body. We were welcomed at Fitzgerald's, who got a supper ready for us … We had scarcely sat down to supper when (Mossie) McGrath rushed in to warn us that the military were coming across the fields in our direction. Breen jumped to his feet, quenched all the lights in the house and called on me to lead him, as I would know the country better than any of the rest. I led the column men through a gorse field at the back of the house in the opposite direction to which we had learned that the troops were coming, over to a by-road and then down a boreen across the Tonogue River.

'Having reached this point, I felt I had them quite safe. I was more concerned about Breen than anyone else at this time knowing that his capture would be looked upon as a major achievement by the enemy but we felt safe at this point where we were about three-quarters of a mile from the Fitzgerald's house.'

Mossie McGrath confirmed Ryan's assessment of Breen's importance: 'Dan Breen came from brigade HQ to get the column in shape for the work ahead. From "A" Company we proceeded to "B" Company … There being strong military centres in Cahir and Clonmel, posting of scouts was carefully observed. The posting of scouts had a two-fold object – it was a course of training in military precaution work and every member of the column received his turn at scout inspection work. Thus, members became familiar with precautionary tactics that proved beneficial later during active column operations … Many men were willing to join but arms were scarce and, further, a very large column would not be feasible. In this way many young courageous Volunteers who would willingly fight under the leadership of Dan and Seán, had to be content with company work.'

Robinson had objected to Hogan being put in charge of a column. He told Ryan that if they insisted on handing over their column to Hogan, they might live to regret it. He said that Hogan was too young for the job. By early 1921, Hogan's subordinates were starting to share Robinson's doubts.

'A number of us were very dissatisfied with Hogan's leadership,' Thomas Ryan admitted. 'There were about twelve or fourteen of the column who wanted me to take over the leadership because they felt that Hogan was lacking in common sense and we were tired of being continuously hunted. Being surrounded every now and then and getting out of these difficulties, more by good luck than generalship, had a demoralising effect on the column and we wanted to take the initiative in action of our own making … Hogan's attitude appeared to be that so long as the column continued to exist and did not lose any men or arms, it continued to be a thorn in the side of the enemy and so served its purpose. But a number of us had different views and wanted to take more positive action.'

Nevertheless, Hogan remained in charge of his column and, by the time the Truce came about in July 1921, they had failed to pull off even one successful ambush.

Organising now took up all of Robinson's time. Cut off from day-to-day Volunteer life at the Rosegreen HQ, he ceased to have any real influence. Augusteijn says: 'The fighting men gradually lost their respect for him as he now rarely did any fighting himself. The local men considered him a thorn in their side with his relentless requests and his criticism of their lack of action, while GHQ was rarely satisfied with his work. The column men as a rule had very little respect for those who were not involved in the fighting.'

Thomas Ryan came to regret aspects of the manner in which Robinson was treated as the war approached its end: 'With the wisdom of later years, I realise that had he been possessed of a more forceful character and spent more of his time with the columns, where he might have influenced or directed their activities on the spot, we might have had less to lament in the way of lost opportunities.'

Breen took time out from fighting to marry Brigid Malone, a member of a prominent Dublin republican family, on 12 June 1921. She had nursed him back to good health in her mother's home when he was injured during the attempted assassination of Lord French.

Immortalised in a series of fascinating photographs, the 'on the run' wedding ceremony took place in splendid circumstances at Glengat House, six miles outside Clonmel. The Breens were joined for the celebrations by leading lights from the brigade such as Hogan, Jerome Davin and Dinny Lacey. Hogan was Breen's best man. As Breen put it in *My Fight for Irish Freedom*, he married 'in the front line of battle'.

A Breen family friend said: 'I think the marriage was a bit of a disaster, though they kept up appearances. Mrs Breen was a member of a family who were what we would call republican aristocracy. All belonging to her had been out in 1916 and so forth. When she married Dan, she thought that she was marrying a "Hero of the Revolution". After Dan went into politics she imagined that he'd go far, that he'd end up being a government minister or the likes. Her friends were all married to men who became cabinet members or held other positions of importance in the new dispensation. Dan was just too wild for that kind of thing, a loose cannon, and Dev never quite trusted him. Too many things had happened to Dan when he was young for him to ever settle down to normal family life. And then there were the circumstances in which the marriage took place. He was one of the most wanted men in the country on the morning that they got married. A few weeks later there was the Truce and Dan was off to America. Then came the Civil War and Dan was away in the mountains, more of a wanted man that he'd ever been during the fight against the British. Then he got locked up. Then he was away in America again. To top it all off, he blotted his copybook with Dev. I don't think Dev was too impressed with his drinking and gambling ways. She had high hopes but they were dashed … Now, Dan had a heart of gold and he was lovely person, but I don't think he can have been a great husband. Being a hero is a tricky business. Living with a hero must have been twice as tricky.'

Paddy O'Dwyer spent some typically memorable time with Breen after his marriage and just before the Truce. He saw at close quarters why Breen was held in such affection by the same fighting men who were alienated from Robinson: 'A scout reported to Breen that a party of British troops, about fifty strong, was on the road near the Cross of Donohill. Breen took [James] O'Gorman and myself with him and we went towards the cross. Near the chapel of Donohill we met another scout, who told us that the military – a cyclist party – were holding up people on the Tipperary Road which was about two fields away. As we approached the road, Breen told O'Gorman to take cover and to fire at anything he saw with a uniform on it. I got a presentiment that Breen intended to attack the troops single-handed, in his native place of Donohill and within sight of his house. He wanted me to keep back, but I followed him to the road. The troops had, fortunately, disappeared as suddenly as they'd appeared.'

As peace and the possibility of a deal loomed, Dan Breen seemed to have lots of fight left in him but, in fact, his fighting days were nearly over. He would henceforth distinguish himself, not as a warrior, but as a peacemaker.

15

THE TRUCE

The majority have no right to do wrong.

Eamon De Valera

The Truce was agreed on 11 July 1921. The IRA was to retain its arms and the British army was to remain in barracks for the duration of peace negotiations. Many IRA officers interpreted the Truce as a temporary break in the fighting. They continued to recruit and to train volunteers. Some reports suggested that the IRA had over 72,000 men at its disposal by the first months of 1922. The brave hearts that joined the IRA once the fighting stopped were called Truceleers.

Breen took the opportunity provided by the Truce to travel freely through south Tipperary for the first time since 1919. Roving from one end of the county to the other by pony and trap, accompanied by brigade pals Maurice Crowe and Bill Quirke, his journey was something of a lap of honour. He was greeted wherever he went by supportive followers and acquaintances.

He also felt the pulse of the populous and, by undertaking such a flamboyant journey, gave the first indication that the rest of his life might be that of a public man.

Bill Quirke, a brigade intelligence officer, enjoyed a reputation for being one of the most glamorous officers in the IRA. He and Breen were lifelong buddies. When Quirke died in

1955, Breen was one of the pallbearers at his funeral.

At some stage during that late summer trip, the horse pulling the three men bolted, causing Breen to be thrown from the trap. It took Quirke and Crowe some time to get their vehicle under control and, when they finally got back to Breen, they found the national hero spread-eagled on the ground and seemingly dead.

'Is he dead?' Maurice Crowe enquired.

'He is,' Quirke said forlornly, having a fair idea that Breen was bluffing. 'And it's a terrible tragedy that Dan Breen should die this way after all his years of fighting the British. He died in an accident, after winning Ireland's freedom.'

Quirke stared at Breen for a second and then he looked over to Crowe: 'Why don't we put a couple of bullets into him and put the story about that he fell defending himself against the British? We could give him a hero's funeral.'

This brought a swift end to Breen's bluff, as he sat up straight. 'Aye, you bastard,' he retorted to Quirke, smiling, 'and no better man to do it either.'

In September 1921, Breen headed for Dublin. The Treaty negotiated by a team led by Collins and Arthur Griffith was signed on 6 December. The most contentious aspect of the deal, for unadulterated republicans like Breen and Cork IRA boss, Liam Lynch, was the effective abolition of the Irish Republic declared in 1916 and reiterated in 1919. The Treaty gave Ireland the status of a dominion within the British Commonwealth, enjoying a relationship to Britain similar to that enjoyed by Canada. The British monarch would be the head of state. The British retention of so-called Treaty Ports and the partition of the island seemed like lesser evils, though partition caused more southern anxiety than is generally acknowledged.

Breen left Dublin and returned to Tipperary when the implications of the Treaty became known. On 7 December, he held a meeting with Seán Hogan, Liam Lynch and other IRA officers opposed to the new accord. He urged Lynch – who became the leader of the IRA during the approaching Civil War – to recommence the fighting but, when nothing happened and when he noted a palpable appetite for peace amongst the people, he headed for America. His trip was not some sort of disillusioned exile; he went to the United States to raise funds for the IRA campaign which few regarded as being over. He was also there to purchase arms.

Before he left the country, on 19 December, he wrote a letter to Seán Mac Eoin, the pro-Treaty Longford man who was both an IRA chief and a member of An dáil: 'You are reported to have stated today in an dáil that this Treaty brings the freedom that is necessary and for which we are all ready to die. You are also reported to have previously stated that this Treaty gives you what you and your comrades fought for. As one of your comrades I state emphatically that I would have never handled a gun or fired a shot, nor would I have asked any of my comrades, many of whom fell in the battlefield, to raise a hand to obtain this Treaty.

'Let me remind you that this day is the second anniversary of Martin Savage's death. Do you suppose that he sacrificed his life in attempting to kill the British governor-general in order to make room for another British governor-general?

'I take no party's side but I will stand by our old principle of complete separation and entire independence.'

In the fraught months ahead there were many similar public missives involving Breen. The fact that this once overtly silent character was now effectively issuing edicts and seeking to influence public opinion marked a substantial change in his style. He was one of the first of the hard-liner gunmen to enter politics. Within a decade he would be an entirely political, as opposed to a military, figure.

The Third Tipperary Brigade was vocal during the dáil debates which took place between December 1921 and January 1922. Séamus Robinson had been a Sinn Féin TD since 1921 and, naturally, he had a great deal to say about the Treaty and its signatories. His bitter attack on Michael Collins caused disruptions in the chamber: 'Arthur Griffith has called Collins "the man who won the war". The press has called him the commander-in-chief of the I.R.A. He has been called "a great exponent of guerrilla warfare" … There are stories going round Dublin of fights he had all over the city – the Custom House in particular … What positions exactly did Michael Collins hold in the army? … Did he ever take part in any armed conflict in which he fought by shooting; the number of such battles or fights; in fact, is there any authoritative record of his having ever fired a shot for Ireland at an enemy of Ireland?'

Breen, accompanied by Seán Hogan, travelled to the United States via London and Montreal. According to *My Fight for Irish Freedom* he met up with Ghandi while passing through London. This seems deeply improbable unless the Indian leader made a secret unrecorded trip to the English capital at this time. A more plausible yarn suggested that efforts were made in London to recruit this now-famous gunman to the cause of Abdel Krim, the Riffian leader who'd established an independent state in the Rif Mountains of Morocco. Krim was busy fighting Morocco's Spanish occupiers, having established what he regarded as a real country with a flag and a name. Such a struggle was very much to Breen's taste – and the people of the Rif were in many ways similar to the community from which he sprang – but he was being recruited as a mercenary gun for hire. He soon found out that Krim's London agent was also hiring former Black and Tans for the North African war. Breen couldn't see himself fighting alongside former Tans, no matter how noble the cause.

In America, Breen and Hogan were reunited with Ned O'Brien, one of the Knocklong rescuers who'd been exiled to America because of his role in that affair. They also spent time with Joe McGarrity, lynchpin of Irish-American support for the IRA. They went to Menlo Park, a small California city which had, during the Great War, developed into an important American military base. The opportunity to purchase guns or ammunition would seem to have been the attraction of Menlo Park.

As things began to heat up back in Ireland, Breen received a telegram from a worried Liam Lynch, asking him to come home as soon as he could. By the time Hogan and Breen were smuggled into Cobh in March 1922, the country was unravelling and the drift towards civil war was clear.

The pro-Treaty dáil had established a Provisional Government and the Provisional authorities were enthusiastically building a proper army, partially equipped by the British. They sought to rule over a twenty-six county Irish Free State. Richard Mulcahy was appointed minister for defence and put in charge of this new force, the National Army.

De Valera, opposing the Treaty, resigned as president of

the dáil. On 16 January, the first IRA division – the Second Southern Division led by Ernie O'Malley – repudiated the authority of GHQ. On 18 February, Thomas Malone (Seán Forde) in Limerick issued a communiqué stating that: 'We no longer recognise the authority of the present head of the army and renew our allegiance to the existing Irish Republic.'

As the British army pulled out of Ireland, barracks were taken over by local IRA units, some pro-Treaty and some opposed. This led to substantial skirmishes and minor hostilities. Breen's first mission, on his return to Ireland, was to go to Limerick where an aggressive stand-off involving mercurial personalities such as Mick Brennan (pro-Treaty) and Ernie O'Malley (anti-Treaty) looked like boiling over. Breen, along with Liam Lynch, De Valera, Richard Mulcahy and countless other national players strove to prevent hostilities breaking out.

By April, the IRA was occupying Dublin's Four Courts, determined to make a 1916-style grand gesture in defence of the republican ideal. The approaching split caused real despondency on both sides. The dark mood of the republicans was well reflected in Ernie O'Malley's recall, in *The Singing Flame*, of time spent in Dublin with Liam Lynch and Séamus Robinson. 'Liam Lynch was square and determined looking. He tightened his pince-nez glasses as he muttered, "My God, it's terrible, terrible."

'Séamus Robinson was dogged. His hair was tousled. He held his clenched fist underneath his underlip. Somehow he had sensed that one day something would go wrong. There was an old antagonism between Mulcahy and himself. Séamus had too much of the French kind of inquiring, critical logic.

'I sat there white-faced, feeling as if I would like to cry.'

Arthur Griffith, the new president of the dáil, could only

address a meeting in Sligo under armed guard. During April and May fruitless efforts were made to establish some sort of pact which could avoid the conflict which was now staring everybody in the face.

Breen was deeply involved in the only initiative which ever looked like avoiding trouble. On 1 May, he was one of the most prominent IRA officers to sign what became known as the Army Document. Endorsed by five pro-Treaty and five anti-Treaty major IRA figures – including Collins, Breen, Mulcahy and Florrie O'Donoghue – the statement said that war seemed all the time more inevitable and that such a war would be a calamity which would leave Ireland broken for generations to come:

> To avert the catastrophe, we believe that a closing of the ranks all round is necessary.
>
> We suggest to all leaders, army and political and to all citizens and soldiers of Ireland, the advisability of a union of forces on the basis of the acceptance and utilisation of our present national position in the best interests of Ireland; we require that nothing shall be done that would prejudice our position or dissipate our forces.
>
> We feel that on this basis alone can the situation best be faced, viz:
>
> 1. The acceptance of the fact – admitted by all sides – that the majority of the people of Ireland are willing to accept the Treaty.
>
> 2. An agreed election with a view to
>
> 3. Forming a government which will have the confidence of the whole country.
>
> 4. Army unification on this basis.

This partial shift in attitude was, from a republican perspective, deviant thinking on the part of Breen and the others. Conversely, it was equally unorthodox behaviour on the part of government members like Mulcahy and Collins, who was minister for finance in the new administration. Acting as supposed commonwealth rulers, they were making a pact with rebels who sought the destruction of that connection.

One republican paper, *The Plain People*, said that Breen was a Judas who hadn't even received his thirty pieces of silver. In *The Singing Flame*, Ernie O'Malley angrily recalled: 'Another little crisis occurred. Some of our officers, including Seán O'Hegarty from Cork and Dan Breen, had entered into negotiations with Mulcahy. A statement was published in the press which was signed by both groups, appealing for a unification of the army on the basis of the acceptance of the Treaty. Our officers had no authority from the executive to negotiate. They evidently meant to work the Treaty and allow the army to gain strength until it could declare for independence. They could not substantiate any agreement arrived at and their action tended to show how disorganised we were and how individual attempts at a settlement would whittle away our resistance. No action was taken by Liam Lynch at this breach of discipline.'

The anti-Treaty men who signed up to the Army Document did not, in any way, represent the IRA. Neither, in all likelihood, was their plan likely to win universal approval from the IRA rank and file. Iconic names like Michael Collins and Dan Breen, nevertheless, still had a touch of magic about them. The initiative did take root and was gratefully grasped by a pro-Treaty dáil anxious for peace. De Valera was equally enthusiastic.

The dáil agreed, on 3 May, to see an 'army deputation' made up of signatories of the Army Document. Breen made his first appearance in the dáil as a non-elected private citizen, a member of a suddenly disorganised and disillusioned IRA.

Parliaments are naturally disinclined to invite active members of armies – of any hue – into their chambers. Eoin MacNeill, who chaired the session, commented: 'Is there any suggestion as to what course the discussion ought to take? It is unprecedented.'

Arthur Griffith, encouraging the dáil to hear the delegation, said: 'The time is one of grave national emergency and it is of the first importance that these officers should be heard.'

It was decided that Seán O'Hegarty, commandant of the Cork No. 1 Brigade, would speak on behalf of the others. His speech gave some hint of the frantic backroom negotiations which had preceded their initiative: 'I have been in Dublin for perhaps three weeks and almost continually in that time public and private efforts were made to bring the two parties here together on some basis. They all failed. I was here myself last week at two meetings of the dáil. What did I find? I found an atmosphere of absolute hostility, personalities indulged in across the room and a sense to me of utter irresponsibility as to what the country was like and the conditions in it … It was only when I realised that it was impossible for the leaders themselves to come to any agreement or, in fact, as I believed, to meet on any basis, that I as a humble individual endeavoured to do what I could. I met Mr Michael Collins on Friday and we talked over the situation generally. I met him again on Saturday with one other signatory to that statement – himself and Mr Mulcahy – and we agreed that we would get together half a dozen men on each side – unofficially, as I took it – to endeavour to come to some agreement upon what appeared to me and to every man who signed that statement a condition appalling to contemplate. I think at the meeting it was I who suggested that a public statement be made and a statement was drafted by two of the signatories, two who have been associated with the anti-Treaty side.'

The plan was generally well received but the IRA director of purchases, Liam Mellows, spoke for the faction which was unimpressed: 'This to me is plainly another political dodge. It is not an attempt to gain unification of the army, because the basis upon which unification is urged is not a basis that is going to secure unity in the army … the cause of disunity in the country and in the army was the signing of the Treaty and so long as that Treaty remains, as long as it is tried to be forced down the throats of people who will not become British subjects, so long you cannot hope for unity either in the army or in the country.'

O'Hegarty responded that two members of the IRA delegation were Dan Breen and Tom Hales from Cork, who, 'were the first two men to start the fight and I will say this, that the suggestion made here that this document which appeared in the papers is a political dodge, is an infamous one and it should be withdrawn. This is an honest attempt to settle a situation that is drifting to disaster.'

The drift towards disaster needed the immediate attention of Breen the following day. Yet another volatile confrontation was now developing in Kilkenny concerning control of former British quarters. In his speech to the dáil, O'Hegarty had spoken emotionally of hundreds of men already being dead as a result of sporadic violence and mentioned, 'another appalling condition of affairs down in Kilkenny, where another big battle is raging. What is the cause of it? One party sent down troops to try and put the republicans out of Kilkenny.'

Breen led a delegation of IRA officers to Kilkenny. They met in the Imperial Hotel with J. T. Prout, the Kilkenny mayor who would, very soon, become the Third Tipperary Brigade's conquering enemy in the Civil War. While the meeting was going on, Provisional Government troops were brusquely dislodging IRA men from an RIC barracks a few miles outside the city. An uneasy ceasefire was put in place but real war would not be long delayed.

The Army Document initiative led directly to a formal pact between De Valera and Collins. Fresh elections were called for 16 June. The idea was that both sides in the dispute would put forward a jointly agreed panel of Sinn Féin nominees, either for or against the Treaty. The contenders would be designated Coalition Republican or Coalition Treaty. Collins, under pressure from the British, repudiated the deal two days before the election but Dan Breen went before the Waterford/Tipperary East electorate, for the very first time, as a joint Coalition Republican/Coalition Treaty candidate. Michael Laffan, in *The Resurrection of Ireland*, says that Breen was 'courted by both sides and his name was the only one to feature on both panel lists'. The idea was that Breen would take the place of Frank Drohan from Clonmel, who had been unceremoniously booted out of public life because the IRA was unhappy with him.

'The Treatyites secured the honour of paying Breen's nomination expenses,' Laffan says, 'but this proved to have been a dubious achievement when he took up arms against them a month later.'

On the campaign trail Breen 'invited' various independent candidates to withdraw from the race in the interests of national unity. One Farmer's Party candidate was invited to withdraw while being besieged in his house for hours by a group of armed men. Eventually he was wounded by a gunshot and, when he tried to leave home to go to hospital, he was abducted. He subsequently accepted Breen's invitation to withdraw.

When the Farmer's Party held a convention in the lead up to the election, Breen asked permission to address the gathering. M. R. Heffernan, the local Farmer's Party big wig, reported in the Clonmel *Nationalist* that, 'Comdt Breen guaranteed that he would take personal responsibility for seeing that the government took every step for the preservation of life and property. He stated that he would place himself at the head of an auxiliary force which would see that strict adherence to law and order was maintained throughout the country.

'Taking into account Comdt Breen's well known reputation as a peace-maker and the great results he had already achieved in the direction of producing harmony between the contending sides in our national parliament, we agreed to withdraw our candidates.'

The Labour Party man, however, was having none of this. He announced that he was 'not afraid of Dan Breen or of his gun levelled at my temple'.

When some Tipperary republicans decided that they would not permit elections to be held in their county, the Provisional Government authorised Breen to calm them down. Laffan describes this decision on the part of the government as 'a remarkable act of faith'.

On 28 June, at 4 a.m., the Provisional Government's army attacked the republican forces occupying the Four Courts. The Civil War began.

Shortly before this, Eamon O'Duibhir met up with Michael Collins for the last time: 'He said jocosely to me, "Eamon, do you know what was the worst thing you ever did in your life?" I told him I could not pick one out of the many and then he said, "Bringing Séamus Robinson to Tipperary".'

16

THE CIVIL WAR

The Civil War was bad but it saved us this much – it saved us from the government of Maynooth. The people were split on the issue of the Treaty but the hierarchy went out and attacked the Republic, threw bell, book and candle at it in every pulpit in the country. And they drove one half of the people against them with the result that they never regained the power they once had.

Dan Breen

On 29 June 1922 – the day after the attack on the Four Courts – the anti-Treaty IRA executive issued a declaration asserting that 'our rightful cause is being treacherously assailed by recreant Irishmen.' The statement was signed by, amongst others, Séamus Robinson, and it called on former comrades to 'guard the nation's honour from the infamous stigma that her sons aided her foes in retaining a hateful domination over her.'

By mid-July, Cathal Brugha had been killed and Collins had been appointed to head a government war council. Dublin had more or less been cleared of anti-Treaty forces.

Having all but accepted the Treaty when he signed up to the Army Document, Breen drifted back towards the republicans when he saw the no-nonsense line being taken by Collins and Mulcahy. No doubt the ghost of Seán Treacy seemed to whisper in his ear as he watched their vision of a thirty-two county republic fade away.

His overt annoyance about the way things were going led to

an open letter, published in *The Southern Star* on 15 July, which was addressed to those ex-IRA men who were now joining the National Army:

> Comrades – are you aware that you are fighting against the Republic that you fought to establish in 1916 and that was maintained and is going to be maintained?
>
> Are you aware that England tried to disestablish the Republic through a reign of Black and Tan terror? … Are you aware that the death of Cathal Brugha is a damnable and eternal stain on the uniform that you wear? Are you aware that Cathal Brugha died as my comrade Seán Treacy died? No surrender to the enemies of the Republic was their cry. Are you aware that there are hundreds of men who will die as Brugha and Treacy did in defence of the Republic? Are you aware that I did my best to maintain the army of the Republic, but I failed because your section took orders from only our enemy – England?
>
> Comrades, I thought my term of soldiering was over but duty has again called me to defend the Republic, which I will do, or die in the attempt.
>
> Will you stand with me and my comrades in arms or will you continue to fight with England against me?

A group of Tipperary republican leaders issued a proclamation, probably written by Séamus Robinson, signed by people like Dinny Lacey, Jerome Davin, Robinson and Seán Fitzpatrick. Breen, significantly, did not add his weight to a decree which claimed that the dáil, 'having contrived at the creation of the Free State government, has by that act forfeited the allegiance of all citizens of the Republic, soldier and civilian alike.' It accused the Provisional Government of, 'using the army which is the mainstay of the Republic to protect the Provisional Government which is determined to subvert the Republic.' All of this new government's orders, decrees and acts had, 'no binding force on the people of the south Tipperary Brigade area, or any other part of Ireland and as such are to be resisted by every citizen of the Republic living in the area by every means in his power.'

During July and August the anti-Treaty IRA sought to stabilise its collapsing positions by pouring all its efforts into what became known as the Munster Republic, a concept which carried some weight in Kerry, Cork, Limerick and Tipperary. The National Army undermined their efforts by landing troops and armaments on the coasts of Cork, Kerry and Waterford. On 29 July, the Provisional Government captured Limerick and Waterford. On 10 and 11 August, Cork and Fermoy fell. Very soon the republicans were making a last stand in south Tipperary and the surrounding countryside. De Valera, president of an increasingly hypothetical Republic, roamed around from one Munster rebel stronghold to another. Clonmel became, at one stage, the centre of the territory controlled by the IRA.

Breen – with a reserve of over 100 men – reluctantly established his own headquarters at Nine Mile House, on the southeast side of Tipperary close to the Kilkenny border. Far from his usual stomping grounds on the other end of the county, he controlled a virtually impregnable group of dwellings which were surrounded by earthen fences and ditches.

His position soon came under attack from National Army troops commanded by Thomas Ryan, who'd previously served with him in Seán Hogan's flying column. Reading between the lines, it looks as if Ryan's soldiers were reluctant to wipe out Dan Breen and as if Breen was equally unwilling to go for the jugular. He showed little taste for real fighting during the Civil War and seems to have spent a great deal of time, uncharacteristically, keeping out of harm's way.

Thomas Ryan subsequently said: 'A second column under Joe Byrne was to attack on the left flank and Liam McCarthy, with 200 men, was to make a frontal attack, but neither came into the picture. McCarthy delayed, removing mines from the roads and Byrne got lost in the mountains of Windgap. We went from Kilkenny to Mullinahone, where we waited till nightfall before we headed into the mountains. I marched through most of the night and got my men in position, fifty yards from Breen's post, at about four in the morning. I would never have succeeded without this young farmer fellow. My trouble was to extend men along 200 yards when they had little idea of what was wanted. I had hardly got them deployed when a machine-gun opened up. My chaps started belting off and I saw all the ammunition being gone in a couple of hours and the column captured and disgraced on top of that.'

Ryan walked bravely (but foolishly) in front of the machine-gun fire, telling his inexperienced men that they would have to put up a bit of a fight if they were going to win. Some of his raw recruits were 'sticking their heads in bushes and praying for their lives.' They were, no doubt, familiar with Dan Breen's reputation as a slayer of men. Ryan calmed his soldiers down, advising them to be more careful when aiming.

'Anyway, we got to scrapping,' said Ryan, 'guns going on both sides in spells with a lull in between. I'd got such a good position on the bank that although they were firing at us from 5 a.m. to 3 p.m., no one was injured.'

Breen was not much impressed by the fight and, years later, told Ryan: 'I could have shot you forty times or more when you were out in the open.' Although Ryan was not yet getting the better of the situation, Breen decided to withdraw, thinking that no good purpose would be served by hanging on to be ultimately captured.

During the days of Breen's Nine Mile House command, Robert Brennan came across him and remembered the meeting in his memoir, *Allegiance*: 'A Ford car brought us from Carrick-on-Suir to Kilkenny and, though the distance is only thirty miles, the journey occupied a whole day. The route lay through a country which was daily the scene of encounters between the rival forces. We passed through the section held by Dan Breen who, jovial as ever, accompanied us to the limits of his territory.'

J. T. Prout, now a major general in the National Army, began the process of driving the IRA out of his part of Leinster and the south-east. Using artillery and commanding the Second Southern Division of the army, he pushed south from Kilkenny, through Waterford and on into Tipperary during July and August.

By 27 July, things were already so bad that Breen and Dinny Lacey were, according to the Third Tipperary Brigade's own historian, an tAthair Colmcille Conway, 'directed to be ready to rush to Clonmel to support any part of their front that might be attacked. Lacey's reaction to this instruction is not known, but Breen noted on the copy of the letter received from Divisional HQ that he had no reserve left.'

On 29 July, around Carrick-on-Suir, Breen was given further instructions he could not follow and was put in charge of ninety men. Prout marched on them from Waterford with 600 troops, field pieces, trench mortars and machine guns.

The republicans rapidly withdrew to Clonmel, with Séamus Robinson then in charge of the town's defence. He had moved up along the IRA's chain of command, becoming commandant of their Second Southern Division. He played a gallant role in the Clonmel resistance – assisted by De Valera – and also saw action in the defence of Carrick-on-Suir and in the Knockmealdown Mountains.

Breen kept his men on the eastern slopes of Slievenamon, not far from Clonmel, between Kilcash and Toor. The ruined castle at Kilcash had been built to provide a clear vantage point from which the Suir Valley could be observed. Now Breen's lookouts climbed to the top of the ruins and used the castle, one last time, for its original purpose. De Valera visited this republican outpost and was reportedly seen, wearing binoculars, directing troop movements. The position was bombarded by a field gun amid heavy fighting.

Prout advanced on Clonmel on 8 August by the back roads around Ballyneale, recruiting fresh enthusiastic men as he went. The republicans, by way of contrast, were now a small body of exhausted and disappointed men, much travelled, trying to hold lines all the way from Cork to Dublin. 'In many IRA commands,' an tAthair Colmcille wrote, 'there were insufficient men even for the number of rifles available and in many areas desertions became frequent.'

The republicans abandoned Clonmel on 9 August. This decision was made, not because the town was indefensible, but because it couldn't be defended without heavy street fighting, loss of life and a great deal of damage to property. No doubt the Tipperary men involved blanched at the thought of bringing about the annihilation of the jewel in the crown of Tipperary's towns. A large part of what was left of Ireland's Civil War was now being fought in their zone.

An animated reporter travelling with the conquering National Army when they marched into Clonmel reported: 'Amid scenes of enthusiasm, Commandant General Prout with the column of national troops to which I have attached myself, entered Clonmel … the people thronged the streets and gave cheer after cheer to the victor of Kilkenny and Waterford. The soldiers were shaken by the hands and doors were flung open for their welcome. Captain Mackey, a native of the town, had a remarkable reception. He was raised shoulder-high by the people and borne triumphantly through the streets.'

After the fall of Clonmel a prudent decision was made to abandon the foolish republican policy of fighting a conventional war. The hard core of fighters went back to what they knew best, guerrilla warfare. Breen returned to familiar territory, the Glen of Aherlow, located to the south of Tipperary town and Rosegreen.

Ernie O'Malley wrote, in *The Singing Flame*, about visiting Rosegreen at this time when dreams had been dashed and idealism almost crushed: 'I left the Cahir valley and arrived in the old south Tipp brigade centre at Rosegreen. The Davins were expecting us; many of my old friends gathered around the fire in their kitchen. After we had drunk the inevitable "drop of tay", they recalled incidents from the Tan fight, trivial happenings, what we did or said, doings and sayings we had long since forgotten, a trick of speech, a sudden anger and a humorous jest in a tight corner. "Musha, do you remember", someone would begin; then a roar of laughter from the others. Bill Quirke had captured a "ghost train" the previous week near Cashel. A ghost train was an armoured car on railway tracks, driven by a noiseless engine, to protect the line. Bill had commandeered it. "Then he brought the prisoners down here for a few pints apiece." It was good to be back here again.'

Collins was ambushed and killed in Co. Cork on 22 August. He was rumoured to be holding private meetings with republican leaders in an effort to get a ceasefire. An tAthair Colmcille maintained that, 'he was said to have announced privately his intention of contacting De Valera. He did contact Dan Breen, who received a message through an intermediary that Collins wished to meet him. Breen discussed this with [Liam] Lynch with whose approval he set out for Cork to meet Collins. Collins was killed on his way to this meeting.'

'Fr Dick McCarthy in Limerick got in touch with me that Collins would like to see me,' Breen later said, 'I said I'd go on to Hickey's of Glenville. It was an old meeting place of ours and he was to contact me there.

'I loved Collins,' said Breen. 'I would have died for Collins, because he was the first of the big men in Dublin to give us support. Collins would stand by you until the last. GHQ in Dublin often did not back us up, but Collins always approved of our actions.'

'Collins still trusted Dan,' an tAthair Colmcille said. 'During Dan's time with the Squad he'd been one of Collins' most dependable agents, often used to check out suspected traitors within the ranks. Collins trusted Dan's reliability and keen powers of observation. I think that the Free Staters always had time for Dan, no matter how bad things got. They thought he'd tried his best with the Army Document scheme.'

In September, the Free State was instigated by William Cosgrave, the new dáil president and it finally came into existence in December. On 10 October, the Cosgrave administration offered an amnesty to the IRA. On the same day the catholic hierarchy issued a pastoral letter which forcefully supported the Free State, while condemning the republicans. This intervention distressed or alienated many IRA fighters. Catholicism was at the centre of Irish life and numerous IRA and Cumann na mBan members were ardent catholics. Breen was not so very religious; the church's hostility only fanned the flames of his unbridled scepticism. In later years he had a reputation for being anti-clerical and atheistic.

On 12 October, the Glen of Aherlow was riddled with Free State troops and remained that way for the rest of the Civil War. Despite this, the IRA's leaders met there on 16 October and decided to fight on.

The passing of the draconian Army Emergency Powers resolution and its subsequent fervent implementation by Richard Mulcahy, allowed the Free State gloves to come off.

'Rumours of peace revived around Christmas 1922,' an tAthair Colmcille noted, 'and again Breen's name was mentioned in press reports claiming that negotiations were being conducted with him.'

Breen was interviewed for the 8 January, 1923 edition of the *Chicago Tribune* and said: 'I am agreeable to the expressed will of the people and to accept the decision of a general election … we do not want to prolong this struggle one moment longer than is necessary.'

The Observer sent an incredulous journalist to meet him and to find out about the peace moves he was supposed to be involved in. He reported: 'The fact is and I learn it from Breen himself, that while he is as much in favour of peace as anyone else could be, his business is to fight. He leaves peace-making to others. Indeed, when I saw him, Breen was panoplied for war rather than for peace. He carried, slung from his shoulder, a formidable machine-gun and his companion was similarly accoutred. Sufficient to say that for three hours he talked peace and at the end of that time we had got no further than the pious expression from Breen that he and his associates wanted peace as much as everyone else and they would not prolong the struggle one moment longer than necessary.'

In another communiqué to the people Breen articulated his faith in a general election. He meant an election for the entire island, including the northern counties: 'I would insist on the whole of Ireland coming in, even if we had to fight them in. The six counties could have been got in but for the weakness of the delegation which was sent to London and accepted the Treaty … The plain people of this country seem to think that we are not out for peace and that we do not want peace. This is a mistake. Let them remember that we who have fought for five years, under conditions that are known only to ourselves, are only human.'

It was difficult for the people of south Tipperary to believe that the Irregulars, as the IRA were now sometimes known, had their best interests at heart. By January, eleven of the thirteen bridges over the River Suir in south Tipperary were blown up or put out of action. Food was being sent into Clonmel by boat but was intercepted by the IRA. Looting had been noted in Ballingarry, with some shopkeepers forced to provide the IRA with supplies.

Liam Deasy, one of Liam Lynch's closest right hand men, was arrested and it seemed likely that he would be executed. Dinny Lacey ordered the detention of five farmers who were

146

the brothers of the Free State army commander in his district. In the event of Deasy's death, he let it be known, the five brothers would be executed.

Thomas Ryan, who had known Lacey well since their flying column days, knew how to put pressure on his old friend. It was all getting very personal: 'I knew that it was possible to contact Lacey urgently through a sweetheart – Miss Cooney, a flying column comrade of mine pre-Truce who became Irregular and was at this time one of Lacey's key personnel. She was at business in Clonmel and was known to be doing Irregular work. I called to her address and gave her a dispatch to be delivered in haste to Lacey. The wording of the dispatch was as follows: "I understand that Liam Deasy will be executed tomorrow. Should you, following the event, carry out your threat to execute the five prisoners now held, inside twenty-four hours of execution confirmation – every male member of the Lacey family in south Tipperary will be wiped out. Signed, Tom Ryan, Vice Brigadier, National Army".'

As luck would have it, Liam Deasy, having made an honourable deal with his captors, was not executed.

In February, Breen managed the last of his Dan Breen-style getaways when he and Jerry Kiely were moving around together in the Glen of Aherlow. The house they were sleeping in was attacked by one of the many Free State units now combing the area *ad infinitum*. The Free State captain was killed by gunfire coming from within the house.

Breen and Kiely had arranged between themselves that, if attacked, they'd retreat by the back door. When Kiely saw a soldier fall down dead right in front of the house, he decided to attempt an escape through the front door. As he made to do this his gun jammed, the soldiers fired on him and he died by the roadside. While this was happening Breen made good his escape through the nearby woods.

Dinny Lacey died during a shoot-out in the Glen of Aherlow on 18 February. He'd grown in prominence during the Tan War and had become an outstanding leader during the Civil War. He'd organised the counter-attack when Prout took Waterford, was in charge of the defence of Carrick-on-Suir and, when the republicans held no other towns, instigated numerous ambushes in the Knockmealdowns.

On 10 April, Liam Lynch was shot during a search-and-sweep operation in the Knockmealdowns. J. T. Prout personally accompanied the ambulance from Clonmel to the scene of the shooting. Lynch was removed to the hospital in Clonmel where he died. He had resisted all talk of a ceasefire though the IRA position had long been hopeless. With his death, the Civil War approached its end.

A meeting of republican military leaders was held in the Knockmealdowns shortly after Lynch's death. Breen, Austin Stack and Todd Andrews were amongst those attending. Stack prepared a handwritten statement of despair: 'Realising the gravity of the situation of the army of the Republic owing to the great odds now facing them and the losses lately sustained and being of the opinion that further military efforts would be futile and would cause only injury to our country without obtaining advantage and being convinced that the defensive war which has been waged by our army for the past nine or ten months has made it impossible that the Irish people will ever accept less than their full national rights and fearing it would cause too much delay to await the summoning and holding of a full meeting of the army council or executive, we, the undersigned members of the army council and of the executive and other officers of the army, do hereby call upon and authorise the president of the Republic to order an immediate cessation of hostilities.'

Breen, having given the document some thought, rejected it. At daybreak, the men went on their separate ways with very little fight left in them. Stack headed towards Lismore, was captured on 14 April and went sullenly into captivity.

For two days Breen remained in the hills living on little more than snow. His party eventually reached the Glen of Aherlow where he went into a dugout and fell into a deep sleep. While he slept he was surrounded by Free State soldiers. When he woke he was imprisoned for the first time in his life.

My Fight for Irish Freedom, for once, eloquently captured the authentic dreadfulness of his situation: 'From Galbally I was taken under escort to my native town, Tipperary, where I was put through some sort of trial. Next day I was taken from the Free State headquarters and marched to the railway station. The humiliation and agony which I endured during this short march I shall never forget. May the reader never know what it is to be marched, a prisoner, through his native town for doing what he believed to be his duty in the cause of his country.'

The Civil War came to an end on 24 May when Frank Aiken, the new IRA chief-of-staff, announced a ceasefire.

A general election was called for 27 August. This time Breen stood as a republican candidate. He was in Mountjoy Prison when he was elected on the first count. He was finished with fighting. He was just twenty-nine years of age.

17

FIANNA FÁIL INC.

After the Civil War Dan Breen, like the ideals he embodied, slowly faded from the scene. He was still a young man when he got out of prison but circumstances – and his chosen political party – conspired to marginalise him. His approach, up until then, had been ground-breaking and radical. Subsequently, a lot of time seems to have been passed in the bar-room and at the racetrack. There were madcap schemes for making money and lofty dreams of doing great things for Ireland, sandwiched in between sporadic (and contradictory) political flurries.

His later life was a lost opportunity for Ireland and for himself but, before his slow fade began, he had one more turbulent adventure to undertake and one more significant political contribution to make.

Late in 1923 he was an elected member of the Free State dáil but, since republican/Sinn Féin deputies refused to recognise that assembly or to take their seats, he didn't make a politician's living. The innate austerity of 1920s Ireland was exacerbated for those who'd lost the Civil War. They frequently found themselves barred from state employment; to the victors went the spoils.

Mike Flannery, a Tipperary IRA footsoldier, had gotten to know Breen well in America. Flannery was rising fast through the ranks of Irish America. He would, in the long run, found the Noraid organisation which channelled American funds towards the Provos when their campaign was in full swing. Flannery knew exactly what befell the likes of Breen when they got out of prison and had to come to terms with an unsympathetic new Ireland: 'In Ireland following the Civil War we became what is known as redundant. After our release from prison we found ourselves without money or even a suit of clothes to our name. We were harassed by the Free State government.

'The Free Staters would break up our republican meetings no matter what our conduct was like. Those who opposed the new regime were labelled and watched. The government instituted a pension plan for the soldiers who fought in the War of Independence and those who opposed the Treaty were denied that right to a pension. It was a nice amount, £700 or something. Nevertheless, those who risked their lives during the war and then voted against the Treaty were left out of it.

'Dan Breen wasn't eligible for a pension. Tom Barry got a rotten deal, having to go to Scotland to find work and live in peace. As a result of the social and economic injustices of the new government, there was a wave of IRA men who left Ireland, many for a few years but most for good. Dan Breen's health was badly impaired by wounds he'd received during the war and he went to his grave carrying bullets that were too precarious to remove. After the Civil War he had his bad health to contend with and unemployment with a family to support.'

The penniless Breen – his thoughts turning to America – started corresponding with his old US supporter, Joe McGarrity, in November 1923. He'd heard allegations that he'd pocketed money given to him for the republican cause during his Truce-era stay in America. He'd been told that the accusations came from McGarrity and from Luke Dillon, an old fenian who'd been jailed for English bombing plots in the 1880s. Habitual rumours of financial sleaze would circle around Breen for much of his life. He wrote angrily to McGarrity: 'I am sure you will be surprised to hear from me after so long a time. I had intended writing you since my release but was collecting information regarding the slanderous attacks that were made on me after I leaving the States.

'I was first charged with obtaining money from Luke Dillon to buy arms and I turned it to my own use. The second was a statement by Miss Kearns that I was not to be trusted and should be kept out of things.

'I want Luke Dillon and yourself to come forward and prove the charge. I admit getting certain sums of money and can account for them all but deny ever getting money for arms from Luke or any other body.'

McGarrity clearly mollified Breen, whose next – less abrupt – missive contained news of a literary project which would make Dan Breen famous for generations to come: 'Your letter received and I am very sorry if my previous upset you. When I wrote that letter I was very upset over reports that were being circulated by both enemies and some of our own that would be doing better work for the cause if they let me alone. I am after writing you about a book that I have written. I hope you will push it in every way possible. It will do a lot of good for the cause if it is well circulated among the Irish over your side. Also, if it could be published in the leading papers in serial form … but I will hold the book rights for myself.

'I will now give you my ideas on the situation over here. The country is in an awful state with unemployment, no work to be got for the men that are getting released; even the soldiers that are getting demobbed are walking around idle. This state of things is having a bad effect in general. The people are getting into a state of apathy and unless something is done soon I feel our cause will not get along as we would wish it. You will note from past history that our people will not look or fight for freedom.'

The book he mentioned became *My Fight for Irish Freedom*. McGarrity subsequently wrote the introduction for its first edition. Like many an eminent man before him, he decided that writing a book would help put his finances in order. His cash-flow was non-existent. During his two wars he had floated along on a wave of safe houses, supportive sponsors, free drinks and pots of tea. Now he was a married man with a young son living in a country where the recently installed political elite frowned on him. The likes of Richard Mulcahy, conceivably, got in their revenge for the erstwhile arrogance of the Third Tipperary Brigade, now in disarray and, for the first time, eliminated from the body politic.

He got a book contract from the Talbot Press, a stylish literary imprint closely associated with the writings of the dead 1916 leaders. The Talbot Press was a properly organised and funded imprint; its books were elegantly designed, well bound and well printed.

One of the most consistently heard rumours about Breen is the one which suggests that he was illiterate or semi-literate and, therefore, incapable of writing his own book. Breen, in reality, was an inveterate correspondent and book reader who wrote vigorous letters full of rich turns of phrase and potently argued points of view. The literary voice in those letters is the same one which suffuses *My Fight for Irish Freedom*, his many press interviews and his 'Statement to the Bureau of Military History'.

That he needed assistance in completing an entire book is without a doubt – most non-writers need help with their memoirs. Whether *My Fight* is an accurate account of the Tan War in Tipperary is another matter.

While being essentially true, it does support a somewhat lopsided Breen-friendly version of what really went on. People whose roles should have been acknowledged are often ignored, while narratives concerning exactly when and where and how things happened are simplified for verisimilitude. A crude simplicity lends it a universal appeal which survives to this day – the 'myth' of the Third Tipperary Brigade comes directly from *My Fight for Irish Freedom*.

Katherine Doherty, known to all as Mrs Séamus O'Doherty, is generally credited with the writing and invisible mending which brought about the original 1924 version. The O'Doherty clan provided Breen with one of his many safe houses during the Tan War and later saw a lot of him in Chicago, where they were Sinn Féin fundraisers. Rumour had it that Mrs O'Doherty smuggled American money into Ireland for the IRA.

Once his book came out in 1924 Breen was perpetually demanding royalty payments from the Talbot Press. Eventually his exasperated editor wrote to him, patiently pointing out the fact that Mrs O'Doherty was still waiting to be paid – by Breen – for her work on the project. According to Mrs O'Doherty's family, she fell out with Breen because she disapproved of his persistent gambling.

Others mentioned in connection with the authorship of this very powerful and significant war chronicle include Sam Fahy, a one-time teacher in Tipperary town who was instrumental in Breen meeting his wife, and Fr Maurice 'Moss' Browne, a republican fellow traveller-cum-writer who played some part in revising and enlarging the 1964 paperback edition.

Denis Ireland, a Belfast intellectual of unionist background, wrote in his 1936 book, *From the Irish Shore*: 'Reading, somewhat belatedly, Dan Breen's *My Fight for Irish Freedom* and still wondering if Mr Breen wrote it himself. But then if a man really masters the art of firing a revolver, there is no *a priori* reason why he should not master the art of narrative writing … This is war as Homer might have seen it, with the single exception that the Mauser automatic and the stick of gelignite have been substituted for the javelin and the crashing boulder. And the army is as heavily outnumbered as was ever any hero of the *Iliad*.'

While *My Fight* was selling briskly in 1924, Breen was busy on the fringes of what became known as the Curragh Mutiny, an event which turned out to be the last hurrah for the IRB.

Because of the aforementioned reduction in size of the National Army, many officers were scheduled for discharge in March 1924. Some of these demobilised men were ex-IRA and IRB members who'd half-heartedly taken the pro-Truce side in the Civil War out of loyalty to Michael Collins. Some of Collins' old Squad, including Breen's pal Liam Tobin, sent an ultimatum to the government on 6 March. They demanded an end to the cutbacks and that something meaningful should be done about advancing the Irish reunification cause.

Kevin O'Higgins – the acting president at the time – dismissed the rebel officers. Another of Breen's pals, Joe McGrath, resigned from the cabinet in solidarity with Tobin and his cohorts.

On 18 March, Richard Mulcahy, still minister for defence, led a raid on a Parnell Street pub where the mutinous officers were allegedly planning a rebellion. It seemed that Mulcahy acted on his own authority. O'Higgins believed that Mulcahy was linking up with his old IRB buddies to start a mutiny so he sent troops to surround the pub. Mulcahy resigned from the government.

'I was very much in the mutiny with McGrath and Tobin,' said Breen. 'I was a go-between. Mulcahy sent out his troops to round up Tobin and company in Parnell Street at Liam Devlin's public house. He sent out six lorries of troops. He had a drumhead courtmartial ready and had his firing squads picked. He was going to present the government with a *fait accompli* … but he failed to capture them and it was after that O'Higgins sent for him … A child was christened belonging to Mulcahy and the late Eoin O'Duffy* was godfather. They had a dinner that evening and Mulcahy had an appointment in Government Buildings at eight o'clock. So also had Eoin O'Duffy. Neither told the other who he was meeting, but they were both meeting Kevin O'Higgins. They didn't go together but they went in their separate cars. O'Duffy was shown into one room and Mulcahy was shown into O'Higgins' room. Mulcahy got his dismissal from O'Higgins and was told to get out and stay out. O'Duffy was appointed commander general of the army, or some term like that. You will also find that Mulcahy was out of power as a minister until after O'Higgins' death. Who shot O'Higgins?'

With a successful book under his belt Breen soon found out that, like many an author before and since, he was no better off afterwards than he had been in the first place. In January 1925, he wrote rather plaintively to Joe McGarrity: 'I had intended writing to you for some time past but I was hoping from day to day to hear from you before doing so. My reason for writing you this is to know would you advise me to go out to the States, as I am still idle here. I am after putting a very hard winter behind me. My wounds came against me a great deal owing to heavy frost and rain and I could not get proper care when I had no work and no work spells no money. I have now given you my case; let me have your advice.

'I am sure I would be able to pass coal on a boat for a few weeks if there is any reasonable chance of a job after getting out. Unless there is, it would not be worth the risk because if I had to work my way back it would kill me. Even the work going out may do so but nevertheless anything is better than trying to live on air. I don't much mind about myself only for the wife and little lad.'

An aspect of poor-mouth lamentation became part of the post-1923 Breen style. He *did* have indifferent health as a result of war wounds and he *did* suffer financially. Reading between the lines of his speeches and letters, however, one gets the feeling that he thought Ireland owed him a living. Alcohol may have fuelled a tendency towards self-pity and gambling can't have helped his cash flow. Restraint, of any kind, was unknown to him.

'Breen at one time was led into a bar by the other fellows before he had to go off somewhere and speak or something,' said Mike Flannery. 'They bought him enough drinks to keep him from going anywhere. That was his evil – drink.'

There was a little light at the end of the political tunnel. Breen was a founding member of a clearly significant new political party called Fianna Fáil which came into existence in March/April 1926. De Valera had resigned from Sinn Féin in protest at the party's policy of abstentionism. He took many of Sinn Féin's most prominent and talented TDs and supporters with him.

For a number of years De Valera's new party enjoyed the tacit support of the IRA but Fianna Fáil, significantly, was a stand-alone political party without a military wing. It bled the radical soul of the republican movement dry. Men of steel like Breen, Seán Moylan, Oscar Traynor and Paddy Ruttledge came in from the cold, dealing a fatal body blow to both Sinn Féin and the IRA. Seán Hogan and Séamus Robinson also signed up. Prominent republicans who didn't go for the Fianna Fáil formula included Austin Stack and Tom Barry.

The relationship between Breen and De Valera within Fianna Fáil was not good. At the end of Breen's career he and his leader were no longer on speaking terms but he did say that De Valera had 'raised the Irish question out of the level of national politics and made it an international issue all over the world. He put the question of Irish freedom on a footing that it was never on before, particularly in America. I felt that De Valera gave the whole national movement a great uplift.'

Before too long Breen was at the centre of a curious parliamentary manoeuvre which presaged Fianna Fáil's entry into the Free State dáil. Styling himself a member of a party called Clann Éireann he took his seat in the chamber. On 6 April 1927, he tried to get the dáil to drop the oath of allegiance to the British crown. He said that he was 'convinced that there will be no prosperity, there will be no political unity in the national affairs of this country until such time as the test which debars one-third of our representatives from attending here is removed'.

His proposal was defeated and *An Phoblacht*, voice of ortho-dox republicanism, felt that 'Irishmen will regret that he should have overshadowed his other days by this crime'.

When the next general election came around in June, Breen fought for neither Fianna Fáil nor Clann Éireann – he styled himself an independent republican. Tipperary voters inevitably found it hard to see the difference between his policies and those of Fianna Fáil. He addressed a campaign meeting in Bansha and, at the end of his speech, encouraged his crowd to head on to a Fianna Fáil meeting which was starting elsewhere in the town. He said he'd never been, since 1923, a convinced supporter of abstention.

He was defeated, partially because Fianna Fáil did very well. His pal Seán Hayes, the Civil War commandant of the Third Tipperary Brigade who'd been with Liam Lynch when he was shot, led the Tipperary Fianna Fáil team to victory.

There was a second 1927 election but Breen didn't run. Spoiled ballot papers carried comments such as, 'Why was Dan Breen hounded out of public life by the people of Tipperary?' and, 'Shame! Shame! Shame! When Breen was fighting for a Republic very few of the present day heroes were about.'

On 23 June 1929, he left Ireland for New York. In an interview given to the press and published in the *New York Advocate*, he said his future was in the lap of the gods. He stressed that, like the thousands of emmigrants who had gone before him, he hoped to return to Ireland when he could afford to do so. Those who had seen him off from Dublin included ex-IRA friends like Seán Hayes and Joe McGrath.

In New York, he joined the Tipperarymen's Association and a new organisation called Fianna Fáil Inc. Like its parent party back home in Ireland, Fianna Fáil Inc. existed in a parallel universe to Sinn Féin and the IRA. Many members of the IRA in America were active in the new group. One of Breen's first public duties in New York was to attend a gathering of Unit No. 1 of Fianna Fáil Inc. on Harlem's Lennox Avenue. In the lead up to this occasion the *Irish World* said that Breen was 'that famous Irishman whose name is known from one end of the land to the other and who is loved for his deeds of valour in trying to regain his country for his people. No one in America who has followed the fight for the freedom of Ireland by the only method that England fears must have anything but the highest regard for Dan Breen.'

The homage announced that Breen was the type of Irishman who had little to say, but who was available when there was work to be done. If the *Irish World* thought that Breen had little to say, its reporters had clearly not spent a lot of time in his company.

Breen told the assembled supporters of Fianna Fáil Inc. that the situation in Ireland was bad, although the sentiments of the people were changing fast. He thanked the Irish-Americans for the support they had given to the struggle back home.

'I am going into business,' he'd written to McGarrity on arrival in America, 'and a talk with you may get me on the right road.' It was probably McGarrity, a former nightclub-owner, who'd suggested to Breen that he should open a speakeasy. A few weeks later Breen wrote to McGarrity: 'We have taken a store at 716, Columbus Ave and will be ready for business by the end of next week (I presume Friday).' Shortly after that he contacted McGarrity to give him the code he'd need when he wanted to speak to Breen on the phone: 'When ringing up, ask for Dick at McGuires.'

Very soon Breen was taking advantage of his garish newsreel

reputation in Prohibition America where speakeasys – night-club-style venues for the illegal sale of booze – were thriving. Speakeasys were usually associated with organised crime and vice. The men who worked in Breen's place tended to be former IRA men.

'He came here for the purpose of finding a job,' said Mike Flannery, 'and the speakeasy was the only job that he could create for himself. He did well. His reputation helped it to be such a success in the neighbourhood.'

Would-be customers went down a few steps off the street into a basement. They rang the bell, waited for one of the bouncers to peer out and were allowed inside if acceptable. The speakeasy itself was located, not in the basement, but in the servants' quarters which extended through the lower regions of a sprawling, roomy, house. There was a long bar in one room, with tables and chairs scattered everywhere. The local Irish-American community were regular customers; their most prominent member, the profoundly corrupt Mayor Jimmy Walker, was a frequent visitor.

Mike Flannery maintained that 'there was never any trouble with the authorities. The policemen would come in for a few drinks and usually not have to pay … that's the way things were but I have to tell you that one time this young fellow came in and was given a drink; he put up the change right on the counter. "Take it," he said, "I don't want a free drink".'

Walking behind Luke Dillon's coffin in 1930, Breen vowed to himself that he would not end up like the dead fenian, stranded in America, out of touch with events in Ireland. De Valera, planning his return to power, attended Dillon's funeral and met with Breen. They discussed getting Breen into the dáil, under the Fianna Fáil banner, at the first possible opportunity.

In August 1931, he got the news that his mother, Honora, had died in Limerick city. That same year he sponsored a tour of America by the 1930 Tipperary hurling team.

Mike Flannery was active in organising the tour: 'When Dan came here, he joined the Tipperarymen's Association. It was one of the oldest organisations of its kind. The Tipperary hurling team had scored great success in Ireland in 1930; so they came here. They came to raise money. The money went to charitable causes associated with Sinn Féin. It provided funding in Ireland for those IRA men who could not find jobs. Breen favoured this idea as the Free State pension scheme only helped pro-Treaty people. He knew what it was like … When they say that Dan Breen sponsored the thing, they mean that he sponsored it for the Tipperarymen's Association and that the association gave the profits to the IRA. Connie Neenan, Clann na Gael secretary, went along to look after those interests. He had Pete Landry with him as treasurer. I didn't want the tour to go to California at all because of the expense involved; it would have taken up too much valuable time. Instead I felt that it would be more profitable if they played two games in Boston. That would get us more money because, in the first game, the Boston crowd nearly beat the Tipperarymen. I knew that the second game would be a real money-spinner. I was only interested in the money for the IRA and I ran the office in New York while Dan was off on the tour.'

Every match was followed, later the same day, by a social occasion where additional fundraising could be done. Breen would speak at these gatherings, usually about his Tan War adventures, and eulogies such as Fr Columba Downey's ode, would be recited with fervour:

> *In the hardest fight*
> *'Gainst tyrants might,*
> *Your place was the battle's van –*
> *All respect to you*
> *Who were staunch and true,*
> *And who proudly lived 'the man'.*
> *You kept in sight*
> *In the eclipsed light*
> *The cause of Rosaleen;*
> *When the sun shines high*
> *In proud freedom's sky,*
> *She'll remember Daniel Breen!*

By October, despite Mike Flannery's misgivings, the hurlers were in San Francisco. A committee of prominent citizens, including Mayor Angelo Rossi, organised parades and parties. The *Irish World*, under the banner headline 'San Francisco Extends Real Welcome to Irish Hurling Champions' reported: 'On Thursday morning the champions will be met at Sacramento by a delegation from the San Francisco reception committee; at Oakland, also, they will be met and entrained so as to reach San Francisco on scheduled time. On arrival at the Ferry Building, San Francisco, they will present the promoter, Dan Breen, with the key to the city. A parade will be formed, headed by a municipal band and decorated automobiles and will proceed to the Whitcomb Hotel. The principal streets will be decorated with the Irish Republican and American flags and with streamers bearing the inscription "Welcome, Tipperary Champion Hurlers".'

As the tour proceeded, legal papers from Fianna Fáil in Dublin arrived for Breen at the speakeasy. So long as Breen signed them and got them back to Ireland in time, Fianna Fáil was going to propose him for a seanad seat.

The *Irish Independent*, on 6 November said: "'From America to Seanad? Mr Dan Breen's Dramatic Dash". The first declaration by a candidate for membership of the Oireachtas to be made in a foreign country is on its way across the Atlantic on behalf of Mr Dan Breen, the well known figure in the Anglo-Irish struggle. Mr Breen has been adopted by Fianna Fáil as one of its candidates in the forthcoming Seanad election. An *Irish Independent* reporter was informed yesterday that Mr Breen, who has been in America for some years, will sail from New York tomorrow. He hopes to be in Dublin by the end of next week. The documents are expected in Dublin in a few days. They consist of a sworn declaration made before a competent authority in New York that Mr Breen will take his seat in the Seanad if elected.'

A senior Fianna Fáil figure let it be known that 'we will place him at the top of the poll or very near it.' Breen seemed to be back in political business but the signed papers arrived back in Dublin twenty-four hours too late. He had been in Montana with the hurling team when the papers arrived and he'd had to rush back to New York in order to complete them. He did not, in the end, sail for Ireland: 'Dan never actually spoke for Fianna Fáil here,' said Mike Flannery. 'I disliked De Valera. He was too dogmatic and humourless. We would all be cracking up and he'd sit there like a statue. Breen did join his party, of course. I know he was very annoyed with De Valera for his pussy-footing over entering the dáil. "If you're going in, you're going in," Dan said and he went in himself.

'Breen was a man who read a tremendous lot, but the way I figured it, he was not able to assimilate it. He did not have the educational background. He'd toss out a thing without really thinking about it, like the church business. As his friend Father Noonan said "He never left the church - he only thought he did."

'Anyway, back to the election. Fianna Fáil sent out a request for Dan to stand in the election for them. I was thoroughly against Fianna Fáil – they had fallen down on the job as far as I was concerned – and I had control of all mail that was coming in, no matter who it came for. I had to open all mail and decide what had to be done about it. I opened this one which was a request for Dan to return home immediately in order to stand in the election. I took a match to it and watched it burn. Dan's wife knew about this because Fianna Fáil got his address and things from her. She raised hell. But it was a dark secret and I never let anyone in on it. They're all dead now and I can talk about the secret.'

A week after the close of seanad nominations the Clonmel *Nationalist* reported that Dan's health was not robust and that he wanted to return home for that reason. 'I don't know whether or not he had arthritis when he came to America,' said Mike Flannery, 'but he would massage both of his arms a great deal. He had an Irish masseur. He was in pain a great deal.'

In 1932, he finally returned from America to be greeted by torchlight processions in Tipperary, where he stood in the general election for Fianna Fáil. He topped the poll and, when his party formed the next government, he started his thirty-three year stint as a backbench politician. His life of violence, insurgence, uncertainty and drifting came to a final end.

He stayed on in the dáil until 1965, a truculent presence and a thorn in De Valera's side. Dev wanted all of his deputies to sing from the same hymn sheet – the one he chose – but Breen was always, for good or evil, his own man. He supported the republicans in the Spanish Civil War. He broke rank with his party to work with the socialist Republican Congress. He was alleged to have consorted with Nazi agents during the Second World War. His occasional contributions to dáil business were boisterous in the extreme. He opposed the Vietnam War at the end of his public life.

For almost forty years the men and women who'd established the Irish state and who then fought a civil war about its nature, sat in Leinster House, glaring at one another in an atmosphere of acrimony and bad blood. Aiken, Mulcahy, De Valera and Breen all stayed trapped in Leinster House until they were old men. It was all over bar the shouting.

Peadar O'Donnell, the socialist republican writer, had long been a close friend of Breen's. O'Donnell's wife was one of the women who'd nursed him back to good health after one of his Tan War scrapes. In 1934–35 O'Donnell was at the centre of the Republican Congress, an umbrella organisation which sought to unite republicans and socialists. O'Donnell persuaded Breen to lend his weight to the new movement.

Republican Congress activists included members of Saor Éire* and former IRA left-wingers like George Gilmore* and Frank Ryan.* It sought the destruction of ranchers and the establishment of a worker's republic. The Congress' Athlone Manifesto, issued in April 1934, said: 'We believe that a republic or a united Ireland will never be achieved except through a struggle which uproots capitalism.'

On 22 September 1935, Breen chaired a convention where republican and left-wing activists passed a resolution proclaiming the Congress''oneness with the people of north-east Ulster against whom conscription has been already threatened and appeal with special urgency to the workers of Belfast to take over their section of the front against imperialism, firm in the conviction that the well-being of the whole Irish working-class cannot be safe-guarded in an Ireland still held within the British empire and in the grip of imperial banking interests. There cannot be a free working-class within a subject Ireland.'

The meeting gave rise to much speculation that a new political party was about to be formed. Such a party could, in 1935, have had a devastating effect on Fianna Fáil. The party was only getting into its stride and was anxious to be a broad church within which all manner of nationalists could coalesce. Breen was the most prominent Fianna Fáiler supporting the Congress, but there were indications that a number of the party's councillors and local organisers were sympathetic.

The *Irish Press*, De Valera's paper, reported that 'since the last convention moves have been made for the formation of an "Independent Republican Party". A number of leading members of the IRA have expressed themselves in favour of the establishment of such an organisation. Some advocate a policy of entering the dáil and others stand for an abstention policy.'

That was enough for De Valera – huge pressure was brought to bear on the likes of Breen. They disengaged from the Congress. George Gilmore wrote in *The Irish Republican Congress*: 'The pressure brought to bear by the Fianna Fáil party leaders upon their too-republican branch officers forced them off the platform … and many of the trade union leaders, when left without that shelter, withdrew also.'

In 1944, Breen, for all intents and purposes, threatened to shoot a fellow member of parliament – James Coburn – who'd accused him of having bought an evicted farm when its owner was dispossessed for not paying his rates. Coburn was one of the last relics of the once mighty Irish Parliamentary Party – wiped out by Sinn Féin back in 1919 – and had been elected to the dáil for the National League, the successor to the Parliamentary Party.

'I want to tell Deputy Coburn that I did buy the farm,' Breen said, during a somewhat confused defence of his own actions. 'I have no interest in the farm and no interest in land; but in regard to anyone who stands for a no rent campaign or no rate campaign, in as far as in my power, I will see they are dispossessed and I will see that the land of this country is of the same value as the house in city or town. When men have obligations to meet, I will see that they meet them. I make no apology to anyone in this house or in the country for my action in buying that farm. I do not want that farm or any farm; I do not want any interest in land or ownership of land.'

He went on to say that he would hold on to the farm, 'until such time as they pay their rates. I am willing to lose money on it until they pay the rates … I am of the breed that wiped the landlords out of this country.'

What Breen was trying to say about the farmer who refused to pay his rates seems ambiguous. He had a good reputation in Tipperary for settling acrimonious land and labour disputes. His lifelong rhetoric – some of which he had just shared with the dáil – implied that he was anti-landlord, anti-rancher, very much on the side of the peasant and the small farmer. It seems improbable that he really would have involved himself in grabbing land – for his own advantage – from which a farmer had been evicted.

To cheers from the gallery he then called Coburn a coward, causing Coburn to challenge, 'Meet me outside and I will tell you whether I am or not.'

Breen was quite willing to meet his accuser outside: 'I very rarely speak in this house, but when I am challenged I feel I have the right to defend myself. If any man challenges me inside or outside this house, I will defend myself to the best of my ability and with the weapons I decide on, not with the weapons they decide on. If I had taken the care of myself that Deputy Coburn took of himself, I would be able to deal with him as he wished. There was a weapon which John Colt made and which made all men equal and if Deputy Coburn wishes it, we can have it out at any time he chooses.'

Daniel Morrissey, a fellow Tipperary TD, was so distressed by the turn that the discussion was taking that he intervened: 'It is the most lamentable thing that has happened for years and no good purpose can be served by a continuance of what has gone on from the time this motion was moved. Things have been said here today, many of them in heat, that I am sure those who uttered them will afterwards be sorry for. There can be no good purpose in continuing this kind of discussion. It is something we should all put behind us and forget as quickly as we can, for the sake of the dignity of parliament and for the sake of the country.'

One of Breen's regular buddies in Leinster House was Liam Tobin, Michael Collins' former intelligence guru. They occasionally encountered faces from their past. 'I became friendly with a butcher in Moore Street named Walsh,' said Breen. 'I used to meet him racing and I often gave him a lift. About ten or fifteen years ago he came to see me in the dáil. He waited for me to come down and I shook hands with him. Liam Tobin was very excited and he signalled me. I said, "Wait, until I see my friend off." Tobin said: "You are a right bastard! Do you know the fellow you are talking to, he's the detective that was with the other fellow you shot that night in Drumcondra." He never came back after that. Tobin sent word to him to the gate to say he was not to return … Another funny story about Tobin. This happened during the war, 1939–45. I had a car and I used to drive Tobin home … We were on the main Merrion Road and I just missed a fellow on a bicycle. He threw himself off it. Tobin said, "It was a pity you didn't get him." He said, "that's Dinny Barrett, the assistant commissioner of the Tans." It would have looked deliberate if I had hit him … He was an RIC man in Belfast … We used to go to mass at 5.30 a.m. in Clarendon Street to get him but he never came.'

He didn't confine his activities during the Second World War to almost running over old foes. One of his prized possessions was a portrait of Rommel, the German war hero, which he claimed he'd been given by a German diplomat.

On 8 May 1942, David Grey, the American ambassador to Ireland, reported to President Roosevelt on the movements of German agent Henning Thomsen: 'In Dublin, Thomsen, the secretary of the legation, has been entertaining, at the Gresham Hotel, Dan Breen, a former IRA gun man and present deputy for Galway [sic], known to be pro-German and suspected of being on the German payroll. He also gave a party in a private room for some members of the Italian legation and several pro-Axis Irishmen. They had a lot to drink and late in the evening they began to sing "Let us drink tonight. Next month may not be so happy".'

George Fleischmann, a German combatant who'd been interned in the Curragh during the war, was a friend of Breen's. When hostilities ended in Europe, the Irish government let it be known that they were sending all German prisoners home. Fleischmann was one of the many internees who didn't want to leave Ireland. Some of these men came from the eastern part of Germany and faced an uncertain future in a land now controlled by the Russians.

Fleischmann was given parole prior to repatriation but did not report back to the Curragh. T. Ryle Dwyer, in *Guests of the State*, says that 'Fleischmann was friendly with Dan Breen … If necessary he was prepared to hide Fleischmann at his home, but first he interceded with De Valera, who authorised Fleischmann to remain in Ireland on condition he kept his presence secret from anyone in Austria.

Ernie Hogan spoke of Breen's last years in the dáil: 'I got to know Dan in the 1950s when he was getting on in years and I was a young man starting off in Fianna Fáil. I can't pretend that we saw all that much of Dan down in south Tipp but he was a godsend to Fiann Fáil because you didn't have to do a whole lot of campaigning to get the legendary Dan Breen elected. And the older he got, the more special he seemed. By the time I met Dan a lot of the heroes of the War of Independence were dead and buried but, despite awful health, he was very much alive. And larger than life. He was not what you would call a great constituency TD. He found a lot of that kind of thing very boring and why wouldn't he? After the things he'd seen and done in his life. In those days, anyway, people didn't necessarily expect a TD to be always holding clinics and arranging things for them. I think that quite a few people were glad to have the opportunity to vote for Dan, just because of what he did for the country. Frank Loughman had to act as Dan's man on the ground in the county. Dan was keen on the GAA and you'd always see him at Croke Park for an All Ireland. He'd been supporting Tipp teams there since Bloody Sunday. Every meeting you had with him was a privilege. A total privilege.'

In the dáil, as a new generation of politicians began to take over, he seemed all the more symbolic and celebrated. Young bloods, recently elected, made it their business to meet the famous but ailing Dan Breen. One new Fianna Fáil deputy asked him what the secret of his success was. 'The secret of my success,' he answered, 'is the word republican.'

He stood for re-election, for the last time, in 1961. He didn't do quite as well as he had in the past but he got in. The Tipperary poll topper on this occasion was a fresh young Labour Party candidate by the name of Seán Treacy.

'On my first day in the dáil in 1961,' Treacy remembers. 'I got a message that Dan Breen wanted to see me. He was sick in the Mater Hospital and he sent me this note written in his spidery handwriting, asking if I'd come to see him. To me he was this renowned figure for whom I had so much respect so I was thrilled to get his summons. As soon as I could – it was my first day in the house and there were a number of things I had to do – I made my way to the Mater. They were used to having him there – he'd been visiting them with his wounds since the days of the Fernside incident. He had his own room and his own nurse, this woman who was clearly very fond of him and who was used to handling him. He took a bit of handling. When I went in to see him he was intrigued by my name. This was what interested him. I think that he was fascinated that a young man by the name of Seán Treacy had been elected by the people of south Tipperary, all those years later. And he was right to take note of it. My parents were both republicans and I was named after the great hero of the Third Tipperary Brigade. So we talked. He was very poorly. He'd wanted to see me because he needed somebody on the opposition benches who would pair with him during his absence in hospital. This meant that he didn't have to enter the dáil for votes, but could be paired off against me. And he really was in no condition to be traipsing off to Leinster House. I was honoured to do this favour for a fellow Tipperary man and for the great Dan Breen.'

Peadar O'Donnell remained close to Breen: 'In 1962, I wrote to Dan Breen … I said, "Dan, with all this talk about the Americans in Vietnam there should be an Irish voice in the chorus. The only two people in the country who can be called on are yourself and myself." Very modestly we called ourselves the Irish Voice on Vietnam. I went to Dan with a copy of the protest letter we were to hand in to the American embassy. I commenced to read it. He stopped me abruptly. "What are you doing?" says he. "Sure any bloody letter you sign I'll sign".'

18

SÉAMUS ROBINSON'S FIGHT FOR IRISH FREEDOM

Once in power, Fiana Fáil achieved a seemingly permanent
political supremacy. De Valera set about, by constitutional and
resourceful means, dismantling the Free State and the culture
which surrounded it.

The Fianna Fáil cultural agenda facilitated the rise of a new
type of establishment intellectual, one who had either been 'out'
during the Tan War, or who was generally deemed to be sympathetic to the 'cause'. Gradually the country was covered with
commemorative plaques and statuary celebrating 1916–21 raids
and affrays which had involved future members of Fianna Fáil.
Former warriors not suited for high office or cultural distinction
were fixed up with sinecures in the civil service, local government
and the many 'bords' set up to promote fisheries, horse and grey-
hound racing, tourism and other aspects of national industry.
This can't be simply construed as a form of hopeless corruption.
Those who fought during the Tan War were frequently the able
go-ahead people in their communities, active in every aspect of
civic and cultural life. They were also, very often, people who had
passionately optimistic visions of what an independent Ireland
might become and were now free to play some part in attempting
to bring such visions to fruition.

Séamus Robinson slipped comfortably into this new establishment. Like most of the Ulstermen who'd fought in the southern
war he, inexplicably, did little to aid the nationalist population

174

stranded within the Northern Ireland or to bring about the end of partition. Instead he settled into life in Dublin's leafy Rathgar suburb; a bitter, comfortable and angry bureaucrat of the revolution.

One neighbour recalled: 'There he lived on Highfield Road in a big redbricked house, complete with an immense garden, that he didn't know what to do with, on a street still almost entirely full of Rathgar protestant families. He was a pious civil servant, anxious to fit in and to be respectable.'

Robinson had been a founder member of Fianna Fáil and he became one of the party's first Seanad members. He remained a senator until De Valera abolished that chamber in 1936. When Fianna Fáil introduced the Military Service Pensions Act of 1934, aimed at providing pensions for IRA veterans, Robinson worked on processing applications. In order to qualify for the allowance, claimants had to provide proof – in the form of a legal statement or a reference from a senior officer – of their involvement.

'Robinson was in charge of the IRA pensions,' one man said, 'with responsibility for giving out the little bit of pocket money that was on offer. And I believe he was a right pain in the arse to deal with and made life miserable for lads who were trying to collect their money.'

During the decades when his fellow party member was operating a speakeasy in New York (allegedly locking horns with Al Capone), being greeted with torchlit processions and brass bands, topping the poll in general elections, purportedly meeting James Joyce (and Albert Einstein) and becoming a national icon, Robinson harboured serious resentment towards Breen. The main source of his sense of grievance was *My Fight for Irish Freedom*, required reading in early Fianna Fáil Ireland. Robinson felt that his role had been played down, that Breen was taking credit for having started the War of Independence and for leading the IRA in south Tipperary.

This sense of affront was largely in Robinson's imagination. Breen's book stuck to the line that the Big Four were a band of brothers who took on a mighty empire and won. There are many friendly references to Robinson and, given what Breen really thought of him, he got off lightly. He also garnered favourable mentions in Ernie O'Malley's influential and literary (if not quite so widely read) *On Another Man's Wound*.

He may have invested his hatred in the book because, in reality, he was still seething from the way the Tipperary IRA had treated him. He *had* been used as a puppet by Treacy and Breen. The forthright farmers and country boys of Tipperary *had* become tired of his dithering or bureaucratic ways. In the profoundly regional and provincial Ireland of that era, he was expecting a lot if he expected all Munster people to welcome his Belfast accent and his Belfast attitudes.

In 1947, he got his chance to set the record straight and to get some revenge. The only problem was, so did everybody else. The Bureau of Military History saw Séamus Robinson explain his role in the fight for Irish freedom and his comrades debunk his claims.

The De Valera administration, encouraged by the Irish Committee of Historical Sciences, established the Bureau of Military History, whose remit was to collect – either orally or in written form – the memories of the revolutionary generation while they were still of an age when they could clearly recall what had happened. The idea, at the time, was that these testimonies would remain sealed until a reasonable period – perhaps twenty-five years – had passed. Most of the collected 'statements' (as these testimonies are known) didn't see the light of day until the twenty-first century.

Diarmaid Ferriter thinks that 'Fianna Fáil was determined to play a role in how the revolutionary period was remembered, but it was also understood that the project would have no credibility if it was mistrusted or boycotted by Fine Gael ... The instructions given to interviewers were clear. They were urged to steer witnesses away from obvious fantasy or exaggeration, but under no circumstances to induce testimony. If the testimony was being given orally, "copious notes" were to be taken and the notes converted into a coherent statement to be submitted to the witness for approval; where there was evidence of unreliability through "failing memory" or "self-glorification", a report to that effect was to be appended.'

All manner of establishment intellectuals were suggested for the job of running the bureau including Seán O'Faolain, Frank O'Connor and Frank Gallagher but the job eventually went to a solicitor called Michael McDunphy. The full-time members of the bureau were Florrie O'Donoghue, John McCoy and Séamus Robinson.

De Valera was correctly cautious about this initiative. One of the leading lights behind it was UCD's Professor R. Dudley Edwards, a man who harboured contempt and dislike for De Valera and everything he stood for.

Robinson's role was to look after Fianna Fáil's interests. In the course of doing so he had ample opportunity to assure his own place in history. Others, like Breen and Jerome Davin, were equally anxious to set the record, vis-à-vis Robinson, straight.

His statements insisted, again and again, upon his role as senior officer in the Third Tipperary Brigade. The principal object of his ire was Breen, with references to his rival's weight, ugliness, unreliability and incompatibility. Sometimes he was portrayed as a near comic book villain, bug eyed and with grinding teeth.

Appended to the rear of one of his statements was a file of letters, hatchet jobs on Breen, which had clearly circulated throughout the milieu that Robinson, De Valera and Breen traversed on an almost daily basis. The only purpose behind this campaign can have been to embarrass Breen to the greatest extent possible

The result was a time bomb from another era, recently exploded, that was designed to wipe out Breen's reputation and the credibility of his book.

The majority of this correspondence is made up of rejected 'Letters to the Editor' signed by Mrs Kathleen Kincaid, Robinson's sister-in-law. Robinson clearly looked over Mrs Kincaid's shoulder as she wrote but, being a government employee, he couldn't lend his name to such abusive epistles. The fact that they were sent to editors at the *Irish Press* group, newspapers controlled by the De Valera family, ensured that they'd never appear, but that the whole of Dublin would hear about their contents. By appending them to his own Bureau statement, Robinson came close to breaking the rules of the body he worked for; Mrs Kincaid's letters were overflowing with obvious fantasy, exaggeration and (assuming Robinson had a hand in their composition) self-glorification.

In one letter she claims that: 'Dan Breen was never in charge of an organised fight during the whole of the Tan War.

Ask anyone who is a first-hand authority.' *My Fight for Irish Freedom* was 'an insult to intelligence and the Irish Republican Army alike.' Either Breen or Michael Collins were denigrated as a 'paper-manufactured "hayro".' 'Whose duties,' she enquires, 'as quartermaster kept him in Dublin almost permanently?'

Mrs Kincaid wrote to the editor of the *Sunday Press*, having received one of her many rejection slips: 'Your refusal to print my letter surprised me. I phoned my brother-in-law Séamus Robinson. He, too, was surprised – at my being surprised. He murmured something about, "Truth is a noose when it comes to trying to get any Tipperary man to expose the Great Tipperary Hoax. No Tipperary man can be expected to espouse my fight for Irish freedom," he said. "But didn't Dan Breen write that?" I asked. "No, it was Mrs Séamus O'Doherty who wrote *My Fight for Irish Freedom* and the *Sunday Press* is anxious to expose it – for sale".'

Some letters suggest that Robinson deserved the credit for initiating Soloheadbeg and for starting the Tan War. 'There are men and women in Dublin today,' Mrs Kincaid argued, 'who remember discussing with Séamus Robinson months before he went to Tipperary, ways and means of re-starting the fight along the lines that he started at Soloheadbeg …'

Her most extravagant claim somewhat undermines the consensus regarding Seán Treacy's innovative mind and charismatic leadership in Tipperary: 'Séamus Robinson was recognised by all during all those years between 1918 and 1923 as the authority, the beginning, the driving force and the brain behind Soloheadbeg and all that.'

Séamus Robinson came out from behind Mrs Kincaid and wrote a poignant but haughty letter to the Soloheadbeg

Memorial Committee in January 1950 which revealed his attitude towards the way things had turned out for him.

He had been invited to attend the unveiling of the Soloheadbeg Memorial. 'For reasons that seem good to me,' he responded, 'I must decline the invitation. As a member of the "Bureau of Military History 1913–21" I have to be careful that my presence and silence at a function such as the unveiling of the memorial at Soloheadbeg Cross (where I was the officer in command), where speeches and addresses will be made and delivered, will not be interpreted as lending even the appearance of any shade of official authority by me, either personally as the brigade officer commanding at the time, or as a member of the Bureau of Military History, to statements that may be made in connection with the function.' He felt he could not lend, 'my imprimatur to proceedings'.

He explained that *My Fight for Irish Freedom* 'had no authority from the GHQ of the republican army at the time or of the officer commanding the brigade or division' and that, 'on the whole, I prefer Buck Rodgers'.

Having persuaded Mrs Kincaid to sing his praises and to wash as much dirty linen in public as the clothesline would hold, he explained to the Soloheadbeg Memorial people that 'I have never yet tried to sound my own horn, nor have I ever yet attempted to wash dirty linen in public – I have never even complained in public – because I had hoped (forlornly?) that some generous-minded Tipperary man would some day try to redeem what other Tipperary men have done (or left undone) to a stranger who went amongst them out of love for Ireland to do a certain job for Ireland and Tipperary and who did it.'

Movingly, neurotically and obsessively, he thought that

'had I served my country in any other part of Ireland as I have served her in south Tipperary, I would not have been damned with faint praise and worse, for the last thirty years.'

19

A Lion in Winter

As Breen's health declined, his fondness for letter-writing increased. These tended to be handwritten and hard to read. He held his pen in a claw because his hand bones had long before been shattered by bullets.

In 1960, a schoolteacher who'd met Breen when he was a young child, brought a group of schoolboys to visit the dáil. Breen eagerly came down to meet the children and to show them around.

That night the teacher wrote to Breen, thanking him for his gesture towards the boys and inviting him to visit his home. A reply came quickly: 'There is no need for you to thank me for meeting yourself and the boys yesterday. As a matter of fact I love to meet young people and talk to them. I had hoped when I reached fifty years of age to retire from public life and devote all my time to going through our country, giving lectures and talks to our young folk. I feel it is more than ever needed today. I am now too old – I am sixty-six – and I am still in the same position, only worse than when I hit the fifty mark.

'I feel a great lot could be done to save our people from the evil influence of Yankee and English ways of life if our youth got a proper grinding in the things that matter. I feel that the things I want done will never be done, as our educational system is so set that a pass in an exam is more important than truth, honour, citizenship. I won't worry you more. I may upset you and I don't wish in any way to do that. I was pleased to meet you and the lovely boys. I never visit anyone, I live within myself. So you will excuse me. Dan Breen.'

When Brian Inglis wrote his 1962 memoir, *West Briton*, about growing up a protestant in Ireland, he was surprised to get a laudatory letter from Breen: 'Your grandmother would not like it – in fact she may now turn in her grave at you reading it. I only want to congratulate you on your book *West Briton*. You surely got to grips with the real position. It's sad for Ireland to lose men like you – you are needed back here to build up an Ireland not rich but with a culture.'

Inglis, aware that Breen had spoken about the need for the Republic to achieve reconciliation with northern protestants, recalled, 'The handwriting was at times barely legible; he had been ill for some time, he explained and found it hard to write, "so excuse my effort". I wrote back to tell him that I could think of no letter which had given me more pleasure.'

By 1965, Seán Lemass had replaced De Valera as taoiseach and Fianna Fáil was about to undergo a sea change. The War of Independence generation of politicians, taking their lead from De Valera, were gradually retiring. New bloods like Charlie Haughey, Donagh O'Malley and Jack Lynch were taking over. In 1965, Lemass wanted some of the old timers to make way for younger men.

Breen was on his list of deputies fit for retirement but, when efforts were made to track him down, Breen was nowhere to be found. He seemed to have gone on the run again. He eventually surfaced in a nursing home in Clonmel. Brendan Long, an able reporter from the local *Nationalist* newspaper, was summoned for a valedictory interview.

He told Long that he did not mind resigning, but wished to announce it to the *Nationalist* and to the people of Tipperary. 'Maybe I wasn't a hell of a good representative for Tipperary,' he admitted, 'because I always tried to think of the whole country.'

He was ready to retire from public life: 'The Ireland of today is not the Ireland I grew up in. The ball is at the feet of the young fellows … I went seventy last August and I am glad to see the youth taking over. If they would only stop squabbling and get down to work, they could make a great country out of it.'

He returned to a favourite theme, the past slave mentality of the Irish: 'The greatest kick I ever got was trying to get that slave-mindedness out of our people, trying to elevate them from the craven attitudes in which I saw them. When I was young the people were slaves to everyone and they were sat upon by everybody from the time they started. If they didn't have a cap to lift, they'd have to lift a handful of their hair. I detested that. I could never accept it – not even when I was a little boy. I could not and would not conform to this tyranny.'

In the course of the conversation he took ill and had to return to his bed but kept on talking as he still had things to say: 'The world owes me nothing. I had a rough time, but I have no regrets in life for anything I did. I might have messed up a few things or I might not have done as much as I should have but to the best of my ability I did all I could.'

In retirement he moved into a nursing home, St John of God's, at Kilcroney, Co Wicklow. His time there was much taken up with visitors; researchers, writers, painters, TV crews, all wanting a final slice of an authentic Irish rebel. He found himself, nevertheless, with time on his hands. The days of dropping into pubs to enjoy a hero's welcome or seeing old pals in the homes of Tipperary were over. Like all old people, he really was living within himself now. In addition to writing letters he kept a diary of sorts containing meditations on what was happening in the world he was leaving behind.

On 23 May 1966, he turned to two pet hates, the catholic hierarchy and the Labour Party: 'I read in today's papers about the plaque that President De Valera unveiled to John and Ned Daly in Limerick yesterday. I took special notice that the catholic high priest attended. Old John Daly died as he had lived, outside the church. The bishops kicked the dear old fenians out of the church. The Kerry bishop stated in his banishment that hell was not hot enough or eternity long enough to punish them. If there is such a place as an afterlife, I hope he is in it. Heaping on the coal, gas, oil, or electric power, whichever is best used for heating the place.

'The new men in the Labour Party are a very poor type of manhood. They are one and all a gang of chancers with no interest in Ireland or the Irish people. They want a plaque put up by that crowd to the great James Connolly. What an insult to a great man and what he stood for! Connolly was FIRST Irish and he wanted his country free from the slave chains of England. When that job was done he wanted a social system set up for the benefit of all our people – not for the benefit of one section, one party.'

He'd started a love affair with Dublin before he'd settled there. Now that he was living on the city's perimeter, he had caustic things to say about it in his journal: 'Dublin is Dublin and it is still the Pale. The Anglo blood is hard to change. You may change one or two of them but the great majority will always be anti-Irish. They tasted the ways of empire and served it for a way of life – so they can't ever change. The Castle catholic is far worse than the Anglo type. The crown servants are at heart loyal to the English. The bishops and clergy were ninety-nine per cent on the side of the enslavers.'

Diarmuid Crowley, a Provisional IRA activist in the 1980s, visited the old gunfighter as a child: 'My dad was a civil servant in the department of finance and his dad had been in the IRA during the Tan War. Dad was active in Fianna Fáil and was all in favour of anything to do with Irish Ireland … he'd known Dan Breen since he was a kid. When Dan ended up out in Kilcroney he was pretty close to our home – we lived in Killiney – so dad would go out to visit pretty regularly. To bring him books and to chew the fat, usually on a Sunday afternoon. I'd have been about eight or nine at the time and dad wanted me to meet what he called "this great man". Dan always made time for me; he was kind of like a teacher, really. He'd want to explain things. It might be a little lesson on Irish history or something about one of the shrubs growing in the grounds of Kilcroney. In a way, I think, he was more comfortable with me than he was with dad. Possibly because there was something innocent about Dan for all that he had done when he was fighting. I was too young to understand how "famous" he was. To me he was just an elderly man and I loved going to see him on that level. When I got old enough I read *My Fight for Irish Freedom*. It was all right … Dan had an influence on me as a human being … brave and dignified sitting there in his room in a nursing home. Waiting for death, I suppose. This big old man who'd seen and done more than I could ever hope to see or do.'

Donagh MacDonagh, the son of 1916 leader Thomás MacDonagh, was one of Breen's most frequent visitors at Kilcroney. A talented poet, playwright and balladeer, MacDonagh was a district court judge whose best known work was the 1946 comic verse drama, *Happy as Larry*. Through MacDonagh, Breen came into contact with diverse circles of artists and intellectuals. Wexford historian, Nicky Furlong, recalls sculptor John Behan, poet Patrick Kavanagh and movie director John Huston, as people who visited Breen via MacDonagh.

'Donagh never told me anything about his past life, which must have been harrowing,' said Furlong. 'Dan did. Donagh had been born into this world a physical wreck. His spine was so bad, his intestines so twisted, that no insurance company would take him on.

'Dan told me that after the execution of his father, Thomás MacDonagh, various republicans got together and formed the Green Cross, an organisation which looked after the widows and orphans of executed men and men who were killed in active service.

'It was through the Green Cross that Dan came to know Donagh and Donagh became friendly with him. For Donagh, you must remember, every day was a new life. He arrived on the scene full of stories and ideas, the life of the party. He did an immense amount of good for people. He looked after Dan extremely well.

'Donagh used to bring Dan out for some wonderful get-togethers. He was always going to see him in Kilcroney, urging people to go out to see him, filling him in on the affairs of the day.

'A favourite topic was fellows who were doing well and fellows who should be shot. One man for whom they had a particular dislike was Ernest Blythe.* MacDonagh used to report every slide from esteem, statement, abuse, and jeer relating to Blythe with great relish and Dan always enjoyed this, responding with seeming knowledge of the background. Of course he may have been greatly amused at MacDonagh's power of invective. I remember poor Dan laughing one day in the Glen of the Downs until it hurt. MacDonagh was brilliantly able to mimic Blythe, his accent, facial expression and hand gestures.

'I remember Donagh and himself being completely antagonistic to Christmas, the sending of Christmas cards and the whole idea of Christ's birth being celebrated when the whole thing was a fairytale. The interesting point about Dan Breen was that, despite his attitude, he was a puritanical man; a stern father figure who might not let his children mix with undesirables. He was not a loose-living deviant type. He thought deeply about proper behaviour and how it should be enforced.

'Donagh went off to Spain for a holiday. While there he contracted some bug, he came home and in a short time was dead. He died on 1 January 1968. The bottom fell out of our lives. Dan was shattered in as much as a man already broken could be shattered. We made all the arrangements to go to the funeral. My wife and I went to communion and Dan expressed his surprise at people going to communion at night. Years ago, he said, people had to fast before going to the rails. I explained about Vatican II and he said, "I suppose so."

'The next day we went to the burial at Glasnevin. I'll always remember the sight of the three of us, lonely people, with a great friend and a national figure dead and being buried. All the government ministers were around the grave. We kept away because we didn't want to be dragging Dan over headstones and kerbs. Nevertheless – he was there – a giant of the national struggle known the world over. A pitiful sight with the two of us standing there linking him. He was seen, known and recognised by several government ministers and not one of them came over to shake his hand, to say, "Hello, how are you?", "Good Luck" or anything else. We just brought him out for a meal. That was the last satisfactory day out I had with Dan because whenever I went out to see him again, there was always the great absence and the great sorrow – Donagh MacDonagh not there.'

Towards the end of his life Breen returned publicly to the catholic church. He'd always attended church ceremonies (funerals, commemorative masses, etc.) and some priests were close friends but he was a notoriously forceful anti-clerical creature. Peadar O'Donnell recalled visiting him in hospital one day when a senior bishop came to pay his respects. A nurse came into the room to tell Breen that the bishop was outside. 'Ah, just tell him to fuck off!' Breen told her.

In a press interview announcing his return to religion he said, 'A canon – I forget his name right now – an old clergyman came here and we had a long chat for hours. So I decided to resume. Well, I didn't resume to accept everything … most things in reason, believing in God and that Christ was here …'

He argued that he'd always believed in God, 'but not in the God that was put up by some clerics … a God that was terrifying, but a God who was charitable and lovable and that cared for the children of the world and didn't put them there for the pleasure of seeing them damned.'

'I hate the creepy crawling thing,' he said. 'God doesn't want us to crawl or He doesn't want you to humble yourself beyond what is dignified. There was no softness in Christ. He was a hard man. He gave the people what they deserved. He gave them a kick in the backside and told them not to be crying and grumbling and hypocritical. When we were young we were very much afraid of the priests. They were terribly bossy in my young days – they'd give you a clip on the ear for very little. What sins could a boy of that age have except that he stole a few apples out of an orchard? And I don't see that as a sin.

'I see such a lot of shrines all over the country. I don't believe in shrines being put up to Christ or the Blessed Virgin on the roadside because people are not worthy of it. You have to be very spiritual and very holy before you put up shrines. They're too precious, too sacred and most of the shrines are shocking monstrosities.'

Dan Breen was preparing for death. He tended sapling trees he'd planted in the grounds of Kilcroney. These trees, he believed, contained the spirits of those who had gone before him to the grave. He got into trouble with the authorities for smuggling rat poison into Kilcroney; squirrels were killing his saplings and had to be eradicated. He arranged to have a silver tea service, a wedding present, melted down and formed into a chalice for the altar in the Kilcroney chapel.

He died on 27 December 1969. The Northern Ireland troubles were about to erupt. In his last letter to Clonmel Fianna Fáil man, Frank Loughman, he asked, 'When are we going to the north?'

In a final interview he talked about his own death.

'Do you look forward to spring?' he was asked.

'Ah, yes, when the buds and flowers come out and the birds start singing,' he replied. 'Nature is marvellous. We'll have a great chorus of songsters here in a few weeks. There are a couple of great thrushes and they'll be trying to best each other with the singing.'

'And, after spring, what do you look forward to?'

'The long, long sleep. That's the only ambition I have left.

The long, long sleep.'

    'It will be a happy one?'

    'It will be a happy one.'

Appendix 1

Third Tipperary Brigade anti-Treaty Proclamation

POBLACHT NA hÉIREANN

Whereas: The Irish Republican Army was established to maintain the Irish Republic and, having sworn allegiance to the Republic, is determined to resist every power, foreign and domestic, inimical thereto and

Whereas: The setting up of the Free State government is inimical to the established Republic, and the majority of the dáil having contrived at the creation of the Free State government, have by that act forfeited the allegiance of all citizens of the Republic, soldier and civilian alike, and

Whereas: The present dáil cabinet and the majority of general headquarters staff are avowed supporters of the 'Articles of Agreement to the Treaty' signed in London on 6 December 1921, and are using the army which is the mainstay of the Republic to protect the Provisional Government which is determined to subvert the Republic.

- The attempt to set up the government of the Free State is illegal and immoral.
- All their orders, decrees, and acts have no binding force on the people of the south Tipperary Brigade area, or any other part of Ireland, and as such are to be resisted by every citizen of the Republic living in the area by every means in his power.

Séamus Robinson, Denis Lacey, Seán Fitzpatrick
Michael Sheehan, Jerome Davin, Patrick Ryan
Tadgh O'Dwyer, Brian Shanahan.

APPENDIX 2

THE GALTEE MOUNTAIN BOY

I joined the flying column in 1916,
In Cork with Seán Moylan,
In Tipperary with Dan Breen,
Arrested by Free Staters
And sentenced for to die,
Farewell to Tipperary
Said the Galtee Mountain Boy.

We crossed the pleasant valleys
And over the hilltops green
Where we met with Dinny Lacey,
Seán Hogan and Dan Breen
Seán Moylan and his gallant crew,
They kept the flag flying high.
Farewell to Tipperary
Said the Galtee Mountain Boy.

We crossed the Dublin Mountains,
We were rebels on the run.
Though hunted night and morning,
We were outlaws but free men.
We tracked the Wicklow Mountains
As the sun was shining high.
Farewell to Tipperary
Said the Galtee Mountain Boy.

I'll bid farewell to old Clonmel
That I ne'er will see no more
And to the Galtee Mountains
Where oft I have been before.
To the men who fought for liberty
And died without a cry,
May their cause be ne'er forgotten
Said the Galtee Mountain Boy.

APPENDIX 3

DAN BREEN'S 1927 POLICY STATEMENT

TO THE ELECTORS OF TIPPERARY,

I offer myself as an independent republican candidate at the coming general election and I am prepared, if elected, to sit in the dáil. In taking this course I feel that I owe some explanation of my apparent change of attitude to those who supported me in the past.

Never since 1923 a convinced supporter of the policy of abstention, I did all in my power to prevent the disastrous consequences of Civil War. When the decision to fight was taken I was forced to submit my judgement to that of the majority of republicans, to take my stand with them in the conflict that followed and to abide by its result. The end of this struggle left me with no illusions as to what should be the future policy of intelligent republicans.

I saw, as all of you have seen, a national movement which had written the most glorious pages in the history of our country broken and robbed of its force and of its sanctity. I saw the men who since 1916 had united for the attainment of a common ideal shedding the blood and blackening the fame of former comrades in a quarrel as to the method of that attainment. I saw the imperial and anti-national forces rising to power by means of that unfortunate division and influencing the counsels of a government that had turned to them for support. On the other hand I saw republicanism beaten in the field and debarred from voicing in effective form the national aspirations of the people.

Faced with such a situation one thing and one thing alone

could retrieve our position nationally: THE UNION OF ALL WHOSE IDEAL WAS STILL THE IDEAL OF 1916 TO 1921 AND THE DETERMINATION TO FORCE THE RECOGNITION OF THAT UNION AND THAT IDEAL ON THE NOTICE OF OUR PRESENT RULERS.

APPENDIX 4

GEORGE BERNARD SHAW'S LETTER TO DAN BREEN

An undated letter from George Bernard Shaw to Dan Breen appears in some editions of *My Fight for Irish Freedom*. It concerns Breen's attempts to organise with an Irish film production company, S.A. Ltd, the filming of Shaw's plays in Ireland.

Shaw's filmic collaborator was producer Gabriel Pascal, one of the most extravagant figures of his time. In 1938, *Time* magazine listed him, alongside Adolf Hitler, as one of the world's most famous men. Pascal wrote the line, 'The rain in Spain falls mainly on the plain' for Shaw's *Pygmalion*. It subsequently went into the musical version of the play, *My Fair Lady*.

Breen is said to have met with Pascal to discuss the Irish proposal, but Breen seemed to have met an awful lot of the newsreel/*Time* superstars of his epoch. Shaw's biographer, Michael Holroyd, couldn't recall any reference to the affair in Shaw's archive, but the letter does have a Shavian authenticity about it:

Dear Dan,

Get all this sentimental rubbish out of your blessed old noodle. I have no feeling in business. You can't humbug me; and it grieves me that you have humbugged yourself to the tune of £1,000.

I have given you time to do your damnedest to raise Irish capital. The result is £40,000. For film purposes it

197

might as well be 40 brass farthings. A million and a half is the least we could start with; and it would barely see us through two big feature films.

The simplest and perhaps the honestest thing for the S.A. Ltd would be to wind up and pocket its losses. But after the company has been advertised as it has been its failure would be a failure for Ireland. What is the available alternative? First to get rid of me and Pascal. The protestant capitalists will not back me because I am on talking terms with you, and do not believe that you will go to hell when you die. The clergy, now that they know that I will not write up the saints for them, will not back a notorious free-thinker. The catholic laity will not back a bloody protestant. The capitalists who have no religion and no politics except money-making rule me out as a highbrow in whom there is no money. All of them object to Pascal because he is a foreigner who throws away millions as if they were threepenny bits. So out we go with our contracts torn up.

Next, S.A. must cut film production out of its programme and become a studio building company raising capital wherever it can get it, from Rank, Korda, Hollywood, Belfast, Ballsbridge, Paddy Murphy, John Bull and Solomon Isaacs. It is true that the studios will cost two millions in two years; but when they are ready the company will be an Irish landlord gathering rent from all the producing companies on earth.

I can see no alternative to a winding up order except this. I have written it all to Dev; so don't try to gammon him about it; but believe me and face it. When … turned S.A. down with £10,000, the game was up. You all thought

I was your ace of trumps; I knew that I might be your drawback, but thought I might as well have a try. It has been a failure. I apologise and withdraw. Still, ever the best of friends,

G. Bernard Shaw

Sources by Chapter

Abbreviations

Augusteijn: Joost Augusteijn, *From Public Defiance to Guerrilla Warfare* (Irish Academic Press, Dublin, 1996).

Conway: an tAthair Colmcille Conway, *The Third Tipperary Brigade of the IRA* (unpublished).

Malone: James Malone, *Blood on the Flag*, translated from Irish by Patrick J. Twohig (Tower Books, Cork, 1996).

Maher: Jim Maher, 'Dan Breen looks back 50 years from 1967', *Tipperary Historical Journal*, 1998.

Ryan: Desmond Ryan, *Seán Treacy and the Third Tipperary Brigade* (Alliance Books, London, 1945).

Statement: Bureau of Military History Statement.

Survivors: Uinseann MacEoin, *Survivors* (Argenta Publications, Dublin, 1980).

THJ: Tipperary Historical Journal.

Chapter 1

Dan Breen *Statement*.

Ernie Hogan, conversation with the author.

D. R. O'Connor Lysaght, 'Co. Tipperary; class struggle and national struggle' in William Nolan, Thomas McGrath (eds), *Tipperary; History and Society* (Geography Publications, Dublin, 1985). [Information on economic conditions in Tipperary].

Maher [Breen's comments of Seán Treacy's interests].

Seán Dowling, conversation with the author.

Ryan [Seán Horan comments].

Chapter 2

Augusteijn [information on Eamon O'Duibhir, Seán Mac Dermott and Pierce McCan].

Deaglán Ó Bric, 'Pierce McCan MP' in *THJ*, 1986 and 1989.

John Shelley, *A Short History of the Third Tipperary Brigade* (Tipperary, 1996).

Chapter 3

Augusteijn [information on Volunteer recruitment, Thomas Ryan quote, Patrick 'Lacken' Ryan quote, Eamon O'Duibhir speeches].

Ernie O'Malley, *On Another Man's Wound* (Rich & Cowan; London, 1937) [information on Volunteer arsenal].

Séamus Robinson *Statement*.

Eamon O'Duibhir *Statement*.

Thomas Ryan *Statement*.

Dan Breen *Statement*.

Survivors [Thomas Malone quote].

Conway [Mauric Crowe quote].

Tom Garvin, *Nationalist Revolutionaries in Ireland 1858–1928* (Clarendon; Oxford, 1987) [Robinson's letter to Frank Gallagher].

Chapter 4

Ernie Hogan, conversation with the author.

John D. Brewer, *The Royal Irish Constabulary; An Oral History* (Institute of Irish Studies; Belfast, 1999).

Seán Kavanagh, *The Irish Volunteers' Intelligence Organisation* (Capuchin Annual, Dublin, 1969).

Kenneth Griffith and Timothy O'Grady, *Curious Journey: An Oral History of Ireland's Unfinished Revolution* (Hutchinson; London 1987) [Martin Walton quote].

Michael J. Costello, conversation with the author.

Malone.

Chapter 5

Survivors [Peadar O'Donnell quote].

Séamus Robinson *Statement*.

Michael Hayes, *The Importance of Dáil Éireann* (Capuchin Annual, Dublin, 1969).

Tadgh Crowe *Statement*.

Ryan [Maurice Crowe quote].

Patrick O'Dwyer *Statement*.

Dan Breen *Statement*.

Chapter 6

Joost Augusteijn, 'The Operations of the South Tipperary IRA', *THJ*, 1996 [RIC report].

Patrick O'Dwyer *Statement*.

Risteárd Mulcahy, *Richard Mulcahy (1886-1971): A Family Memoir* (Aurelian Press; Dublin 1999).

Malone [Mulcahy's Frongoch speech].

Jerome Davin *Statement*.

Ryan [information on Soloheadbeg inquest].

Séamus Robinson *Statement*.

Dan Breen *Statement*.

Patrick O'Dwyer *Statement*.

Ryan [Maurice Crowe recollection].

Eamon O'Duibhir *Statement*.

Chapter 7

Ryan [information on the fate of Soloheadbeg gelignite].

Tadgh Crowe *Statement*.

Chapter 8

Eamon O'Duibhir *Statement*.

Mick Davern *Statement*.

Ryan [information on Knocklong rescue].

Chapter 9

Mick Davern *Statement*.

Joost Augusteijn, 'The Operations of the South Tipperary IRA', *THJ*, 1996 [RIC report].

Séan Gaynor, 'With Tipperary No. 1 Brigade in North Tipperary 1917–21', *THJ*, 1993

Chapter 10

Maher [Breen on Dublin working-class].

Dan Breen *Statement*.

Risteárd Mulcahy, *Richard Mulcahy (1886-1971): A Family Memoir* (Aurelian Press; Dublin 1999).

Joe Leonard *Statement* [the foundation and purpose of the Squad].
Patrick O'Dwyer *Statement*
Frank McGrath *Statement.*
Vinnie Byrne *Statement.*

Chapter 11
Patrick O'Dwyer *Statement.*
Frank McGrath *Statement.*
Dan Breen *Statement.*
Ryan [Seán Hogan incident].
Vinnie Byrne *Statement.*

Chapter 12
Meda Ryan, *The Real Chief; The Story of Liam Lynch* (Mercier Press, Cork, 2004) [Conference between Breen, Lynch and others].
John D. Brewer, *The Royal Irish Constabulary; An Oral History* (Institute of Irish Studies; Belfast, 1999).
Augusteijn [barracks attacks].
Survivors [Thomas Malone on Kilmallock].
J. M. McCarthy *Statement.*
Jerome Davin *Statement.*
Dan Breen *Statement.*

Chapter 13
Dan Breen *Statement.*
Ryan [Treacy's letter to Cait de Paor].
Eamon O'Duibhir *Statement.*
Jerome Davin *Statement.*
Maher [Breen on Seán Treacy].

Chapter 14
Joost Augusteijn, 'The Operations of the South Tipperary IRA', *THJ*, 1996 [RIC report] [internal dissent, Frank Drohan, Eamon O'Duibhir].
Thomas Ryan, 'One Man's Flying Column', *THJ*, 1991.
Maurice McGrath *Statement.*
Patrick O'Dwyer *Statement.*

Chapter 15

Conway [Bill Quirke incident].

Dáil Debates, 3 May 1921.

Michael Laffan, *The Resurrection of Ireland: The Sinn Féin Party, 1916-1923* (Cambridge University Press; Cambridge) [Breen's election campaign].

Eamon O'Duibhir *Statement*.

Chapter 16

Maher [Breen on Civil War and Collins].

Conway [Civil War narrative, including Thomas Ryan incident].

Tom Garvin *1922, The Birth of Irish Democracy* (Gill and Macmillan; Dublin, 1996) [Ryan's message to Dinny Lacey, reception of Prout in Clonmel].

An tAthair Colmcille Conway, conversation with the author.

Chapter 17

Mike Flannery interview, conducted by Nancy Kersey [information on Breen's speakeasy].

Correspondence between Michael Murphy and Professor Liam Kennedy, QUB concerning authorship of *My Fight for Irish Freedom*.

Dan Breen *Statement*.

Dáil Debates. 6 April 1927.

Dáil Debates, 9 June 1944.

T. Ryle Dwyer, *Guests of the State: The Story of Allied and Axis Servicemen Interned in Ireland During World War II* (Brandon; Dingle 1994) [Grey's letter to Roosevelt, Breen's relationship with Fleischmann].

Ernie Hogan, conversation with the author.

Seán Treacy, conversation with the author.

Survivors [Peadar O'Donnell quote].

Chapter 18

Séamus Robinson *Statement*.

Diarmaid Ferriter, 'In Such Deadly Earnest', *The Dublin Review*, No. 12.

Chapter 19

Brian Inglis, *Downstart: The Autobiography of Brian Inglis* (Chatto & Windus; London, 1990).

Nicky Furlong, conversation with the author.

Diarmuid Crowley, conversation with the author.

Michael McInerney, *Peadar O'Donnell, Irish Social Rebel* (The O'Bien Press; Dublin 1974) [bishop story].

Glossary

Boland, Harry. Worked with Michael Collins during the War of Independence. Went to the USA with De Valera as part of a campaign to raise awareness and support for Ireland. Boland was a widely respected figure within the republican movement. In 1922, he was shot by members of the National Army and died soon afterwards.

Blythe, Ernest. Ulster Protestant active in the Volunteers but imprisoned at the time of the 1916 Rising. Rose to prominence as a Free State politician and cabinet member. Reduced the old age pension. Lost his seat in 1933. A prominent Blueshirt and founder member of Fine Gael. From 1941 until 1967 he was a controversial managing director of the Abbey Theatre.

Cúchullain. Pre-eminent hero of Ulster in the mythological Ulster Cycle.

Fianna. Warriors who served the high king of Ireland in the third century AD. Their last leader was Fionn Mac Cumhaill.

Gilmore, George. Leader of south Co. Dublin battalion of the IRA from 1915 to 1926. Shot and wounded in 1932 by the gardaí. One of the founders of the Republican Congress. Active in 1936–39 as a supporter of the International Brigade during the Spanish Civil War.

Haggard. An outhouse on a farm, usually located in a farmyard.

Irish Volunteers. Founded in 1913 in Dublin by eleven prominent nationalists including Patrick Pearse and Seán Mac Dermott. On 25 November 1913, they had their first public meeting at the Rotunda in Dublin. The hall was filled to its 4,000 capacity, with a further 3,000 spilling onto the grounds outside. The movement soon spread throughout the country. The Volunteers were heavily infiltrated by the IRB but John Redmond from the Irish Parliamentary Party demanded they accept his appointments to their provisional committee, effectively placing the organisation under his control. Four of its members – the O'Rahilly, Roger Casement, Bulmer Hobson and Erskine Childers – organised a gun-running expedition to Howth. Almost 1,000 rifles were smuggled into the harbour and distributed to waiting Volunteers.

The outbreak of the First World War in August 1914 provoked a serious split in the organisation. Redmond urged the Volunteers to support Britain and join a proposed Irish brigade of the British army. This was opposed by the founding IRB-orientated members. A majority backed Redmond and left to form the National Volunteers; these joined the British war effort. A minority, retaining the name 'Irish Volunteers', were led by Eoin Mac Neill. This element brought about the 1916 Rising.

O'Duffy, Eoin. Well liked but controversial, O'Duffy served as a general in the Free State army during the Civil War and was partially responsible for the Free State's strategy of seaborne landings into republican held areas. He was garda commissioner during the first Free State governments. When De Valera came to power he was dismissed and became leader of the Army Comrades Association. The ACA soon developed into the Blueshirts, a movement modelled on European fascist organisations. De Valera successfully saw off the Blueshirt threat and the organisation was subsumed into a new political party, Fine Gael, which thereafter represented pro-Treaty interests. O'Duffy was the first leader of Fine Gael. In 1936, he organised the Irish Brigade and went to Spain to fight on the fascist side in that country's civil war. Following his death, rumours began to circulate that O'Duffy had homosexual tendencies. Recent research has tended to confirm such rumours.

O'Higgins, Kevin. One of the most able pro-Treaty politicians, O'Higgins was minister for justice and external affairs, as well as vice-president of the executive council, in the first Free State government. During the Civil War he ordered the execution of at least seventy-seven republicans and was very much seen as the 'strong man' of the cabinet. He once described himself as one of 'the most conservative-minded revolutionaries that ever put through a successful revolution.' Sympathetic to Italian fascist ideas, he was assassinated in 1927, in unsanctioned revenge for the Civil War, by individual members of the IRA.

Oisín. The son of Fianna hero, Fionn Mac Cumhaill

Pony and trap. Small open carriage pulled by a pony.

Ryan, Frank. Joined the east Limerick brigade of the IRA in 1922, fought on the republican side in the Civil War, was wounded and interned. In 1929, he was appointed editor of *An Phoblacht* and elected to the IRA army council. A founder of the Republican Congress. He travelled to Spain late in 1936 with about eighty men to fight with the international brigades on the republican side. Ryan's men were known as the 'Connolly Column'. Ryan eventually fell into fascist hands and ended his days in Germany where, it is alleged, he was involved in a number of Nazi schemes to invade Ireland.

Saor Éire. Left-wing political organisation established in September 1931 by communist-leaning members of the IRA. Peadar O'Don-nell, a former editor of *An Phoblacht*, was a leading member. Saor Éire described itself as 'an organisation of workers and working farmers.'

BIBLIOGRAPHY

Books:

Ambrose, Joseph G., *The Dan Breen Story* (Mercier Press; Cork, 1981)
—— *Too Much Too Soon* (Pulp Books; London, 2000)
Breen, Dan, *My Fight for Irish Freedom* (Anvil Books; Dublin, 1964)
Brewer, John D., *The Royal Irish Constabulary; An Oral History* (Institute of
    Irish Studies; Belfast, 1999)
Browne, Vincent (ed), *The Magill Book of Irish Politics* (Magill; Dublin, 1981)
Dwyer, T. Ryle, *Guests of the State; The Story of Allied and Axis Sevicemen
    Interned in Ireland During World War II* (Brandon; Dingle, 1994)
Garvin, Tom, *Nationalist revolutionaries in Ireland 1858-1928* (Clarendon;
    Oxford,1987)
—— *1922; The Birth of Irish Democracy* (Gill and Macmillan: Dublin, 1996)
Griffith, Kenneth and O'Grady, Timothy, *Curious Journey; An Oral History of
    Ireland's Unfinished Revolution* (Hutchinson; London, 1987)
Inglis, Brian, *Downstart: The Autobiography of Brian Inglis* (Chatto & Windus;
    London, 1990)
Ireland, Denis, *From the Irish Shore* (Rich & Cowan Ltd., 1936)
Laffan, Michael, *The Resurrection of Ireland: The Sinn Féin Party, 1916-1923*
    (Cambridge University Press; Cambridge)
McCarthy, J. M. (ed.), *Limerick's Fighting Story* (The Kerryman; Tralee, 1947)
MacEoin, Uinseann *Survivors* (Argenta Publications; Dublin, 1980)
McInerney, Michael. *Peadar O'Donnell : Irish Social Rebel* (The O'Brien Press;
    Dublin, 1974)
Mulcahy, Risteard, *Richard Mulcahy (1886-1971): A Family Memoir* (Dublin;
    Aurelian Press, 1999)
O'Connnor, Ulick, *A Terrible Beauty is Born: The Irish troubles, 1912-1922*
    (Hamish Hamilton; London, 1975)
O'Dwyer, Martin, *A Pictorial History of Tipperary 1916-1923* (The Folk
    Village; Cashel, 2004)
O'Farrell, Padraic, *Who's Who in the Irish War of Independence and Civil War
    1916-1923* (Lilliput Press; Dublin, 1997)
O'Malley, Ernie, *On Another Man's Wound* (Rich & Cowan; London, 1937)
—— *Raids and Rallies* (Anvil Books; Dublin, 1982)
—— *The Singing Flame* (Anvil Books; Dublin, 1978)
Ryan, Desmond, *Seán Treacy and the Third Tipperary Brigade* (Alliance Books;
    London, 1945)
Ryan, Meda, *The Real Chief; The Story of Liam Lynch* (Mercier Press; Cork,
    1996)
Shelley, John R, *A Short History of the 3rd Tipperary Brigade* (Tipperary,
    1996)

Townsend, Charles, *The British Campaign in Ireland, 1919-1921* (Oxford University Press; Oxford, 1975)

Valiulis, Maryann Gialanella, *Portrait of a revolutionary : General Richard Mulcahy and the Founding of the Irish Free State* (Irish Academic Press; Dublin,1992)

Articles:

Tipperary Historical Journal 1986
Ó Bric, Deaglán, *Pierce McCan MP*

Tipperary Historical Journal 1989
Ó Bric, Deaglán, *Pierce McCan MP, Part 2*

Tipperary Historical Journal 1991
Ó Duibhir, Eamonn, *The Tipperary Volunteers in 1916: A Personal Account 75 Years On*
Ryan, Thomas, *One Man's Flying Column*

Tipperary Historical Journal 1992
Ryan, Thomas, *One Man's Flying Column, Part 2*

Tipperary Historical Journal 1993
Gaynor, Séan, *With Tipperary No. 1 Brigade in North Tipperary 1917–1921*
Ryan, Thomas, *One Man's Flying Column, Part 3*

Tipperary Historical Journal 1994
Gaynor, Séan, *With the Tipperary No. 1 Brigade in North Tipperary 1917–1921, Part II*
Sharkey, Neil, *The Third Tipperary Brigade – A Photographic Record*

Capuchin Annual; Dublin, 1969
Hayes, Michael, *The Importance of Dail Eireann*
Kavanagh, Seán, *The Irish Volunteers' Intelligence Organisation*

The Dublin Review, No. 12.
Ferriter, Diarmaid, *In Such Deadly Earnest*

Acknowledgements

An tAthair Colmcille Conway provided me with a manuscript copy of his history of the Third Tipperary Brigade, and I have relied on his research, especially that part of it which covers the Civil War. He was an outstanding character, a regular visitor to my family home, and a significant historian of the IRA. An edited version of his work has appeared in the *Tipperary Historical Journal* and a copy of the full manuscript is available for inspection from Tipperary County Library, info@tipperarylibraries.ie. Extracts from the book appeared in the Clonmel *Nationalist* in 1957, credited to Pádraig Toibin, and titled 'Come Weal or Woe'.

The *Tipperary Historical Journal* and Marcus Bourke, the guiding force behind that publication, have brought rigour and clarity to the study of Tipperary's past. A large part of this book deals with activities in that county; I hope something of the *Journal*'s approach is reflected in these pages. They can be contacted at www.tipperarylibraries.ie/ths. Research first published in the *Journal* has informed this book. I've relied entirely on Deaglan Ó Bric's research on Pierce McCan.

I have enjoyed stimulating discussions concerning Dan Breen, and related matters, with many people. Ulick O'Connor was his usual urbane and forthright self; his perspective on the twilight years of the revolutionary generation was much appreciated. Frank Rynne pointed me in the direction of certain historians who've come on the scene since I quit Ireland and history. Prof. Liam Kennedy showed me how a true historian might tackle this matter. Des Farrell bought me a good lunch in the Shelbourne and shared his information and attitudes with me. Michael Murphy, in addition to chatting about Breen and Fianna Fáil, was kind enough to show me some of his research correspondence. Fintan Deere facilitated my first meeting with an tAthair Colmcille, and was also responsible for my meeting Mickey Joe Costello.

I'm grateful to my sisters Gerardine and Caroline, and to their husbands Eamonn O'Meara and Val Needham, for putting up with me (and putting me up) while I've been in Ireland researching this book. My brother Robbie was an excellent companion during the same trips, as was my nephew James Needham. Jocelyn and Lucy Bradell were kind enough to offer me Dublin accommodation – it's the thought that counts. Dr Declan O'Reilly gave me shelter from the storm and was a good historian to discuss this project with. Nick Szegda from Menlo Park Library tried to enthuse local historians on my behalf. Nicholas Allen marked my cards on the Talbot Press Archive in Ireland's National Archive.

While in Dublin I frequently met up with Daniel Figgis, Deirdre Behan, Shane Cullen, Shane O'Reilly, Gerry Ambrose and Frank Callanan. I hooked up again with old friends like Dennis McClean. Brendan Maher at the South Tipperary Arts Centre was, as ever, enormously helpful and constructive. Marie Boland and her staff at Clonmel Library made me feel right at home. They maintain a first-rate local history section. Martin O'Dwyer at Cashel Folk Village was, literally, a scholar and a gentleman.

Paul Lamont is responsible for my website, and for www.outsideleft.com. Mary Feehan at Mercier Press was with the firm the first time I wrote about Breen, and she is still there today. She has shown saintly patience. Mary subsequently passed the baton to Brian Ronan, freshly arrived at Mercier. I gave him a baptism of fire. I consulted the Bureau of Military History documents in Dublin's National Archive, where the staff are likeably reminiscent of James Joyce's *Dubliners*.

Seán Treacy, one of the most distinguished Tipperary parliamentarians, was kind enough to invite me into his home to talk about his Dan Breen adventures. Nancy Kersey did most of the research concerning Breen's time in America, and interviewed Mike Flannery. Nicky Furlong met in the grounds of the Montrose Hotel in Dublin and gave a glimpse into Breen's sunset years.

Many of the people who were around when I first wrote about Dan Breen are now gone. My old professor, R. Dudley Edwards, a lively old coot with a head full of history and mischief, once gave me a taste for the past. Captain Seán Feehan published my first book on Breen (also my first book) and taught me a few sharp lessons about life and publishing. Diarmuid Cronin was one of my best school friends. He burned briefly but brightly and had some hands-on experience of guerilla life. My parents, George and Mai, saw that I got the kind of education I needed, and provided me with much else besides.

Thanks go out to Tavis Henry, Tav Falco, Chuck Prophet, Hamri the Painter of Morocco, Elaine Palmer, Marek Pytel, Anne Foley, Seb Tennant, Spencer Kansa, David Kerekes at Headpress, Chris Campion, Malcolm Kelly, Eamon Leahy, Anna Lanigan, Seán Dowling, Pat Norris, Josie Heffernan, Jimmy Norris, Tom and Joan Ambrose, Michael and Deirdre Ahearn, Ernie Hogan, Kirk Lake, Carrie Acheson, Martin Mansergh, Margaret McCurtain, Brendan Long, Dave Barry, Martin Arthur, William Corbett, Bob Leahy, Eddie Bowe, Mike Flannery, John Ridge, and William Brennan.

The author and publisher would like to thank Martin O'Dwyer for his kind permission to reproduce some of the photographs in this work. Thanks also to Rena Dardis from Anvil Press for the use of photographs originally published in *My Fight for Irish Freedom*.

Every effort has been made to acknowledge the sources of all photographs used. Should a source have not been acknowledged, please contact Mercier Press and we will make the necessary corrections at the first opportunity.

INDEX